FLORAL ARRANGING BASICS

Now that you know what types of designs you'll be creating, you need to become familiar with some elements and terms of floral design and find out what basic floral supplies you'll need.

ELEMENTS OF FLORAL DESIGN

Most flower arrangements contain four design elements; a few examples of each are shown here.

FOCAL: The point or points of main interest in a bouquet or arrangement, focal flowers are usually larger than the other materials. Lilies, roses, poppies, calla lilies, gardenias, and orchids are just a few of the many types of flowers that can be focal flowers.

LINE: Line materials are used to establish the shape, direction, height, and width of the design and should draw the eye through the design. Various ferns, heather spikes, orchid sprays, and ivy may all be used to establish the line within a floral design.

SECONDARY: Smaller flowers or leaves are added to complement the focal flowers. Rosebuds, stephanotis, and carnations make good secondary flowers.

FILLER: Small flowers, tiny blossoms, leaves, or other materials, such as ribbon or cording loops, pearl sprays, lace fans, and tulle puffs, are added to round out arrangements or bouquets and fill in spaces.

TERMS AND DEFINITIONS

Before you select your flowers, you need to know some basic terms and definitions used throughout this book.

•Flower Parts

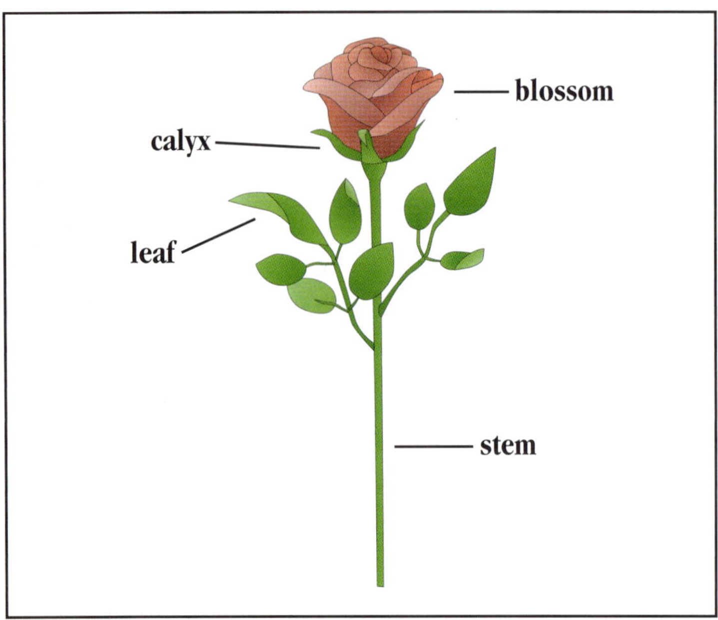

•**Stem wire** is 16-22 gauge and **floral wire** is 24-30 gauge as designated in this book.

•Tape Point

The point at which stems are floral taped together during assembly of hand-wrapped bouquets.

•Sprig

A grouping of one or more blossoms or leaves cut from a main stem.

•Cluster

Formed from sprigs, individual blossoms, or leaves taped together to form one short stem.

•Flower Pick

A purchased floral item made up of several flowers or leaves or a combination of flowers and leaves on a short, sturdy stem.

PLANNING WEDDING FLORAL DESIGNS

On the next few pages, we've given you lots of information and a Wedding Flower Planning Guide to assist in the overall planning of your wedding floral designs. There are few hard and fast rules, and the final decision as to style and color largely depends upon your personal taste and wishes.

FIRST THINGS FIRST

The first thing that should be noted about the floral designs in this book is that they are NOT difficult to duplicate nor to assemble in YOUR CHOICE of flowers and colors. You may substitute any type or color of flower for the flowers we show, provided the flowers are the same general size and shape. The hand-held bouquets shown offer much versatility for you and your Attendants. Any of the Attendant's bouquets may be appropriate for the Bride, and the Bride's bouquets may be suitable for Attendants by changing some of the white flowers and accents to the desired wedding colors.

Our bouquets and other floral designs are made from silk flowers, greenery, and preserved materials. The color range of the beautiful silk flowers and types of silk greenery and dried and preserved materials available today is nearly endless. Silk flowers come in many colors that are not normally available in fresh flowers, can provide just the right color needed, and also offer the added benefit of using types of flowers that may be out of season.

As a starting point for planning the number and kinds of floral designs you'll need, consider these questions:

1. *What time of year will the wedding take place?*
The time of year can help you determine what flowers you choose to use in your bouquet and other floral designs. A spring bride may choose tulips, irises, daffodils, or other newly emerging spring flowers. Similarly, a winter bride may choose poinsettias, gardenias, camellias, or other elegant winter blooms.

2. *Where will the wedding be held? What decorative floral designs would you like?*
An outdoor wedding in a gazebo is suitable for casual garden flowers, whereas a wedding at a large cathedral calls for more formal, dramatic, or exotic flowers. The size of the church or hall may also determine how many and how large the floral designs can be. Be sure to ask questions when you call the church or hall; some buildings have restrictions about floral designs.

3. *What time of day will the wedding be held?*
An evening wedding usually calls for a more formal setting. Flowers such as lilies, tropical or exotic flowers, roses, or tulips can be used. Formal bouquets, such as a cascade or crescent-shaped bouquet, should be accented with pearls, lace trims, and satin or metallic ribbon. A morning or afternoon wedding can use more casual flowers such as carnations, daisies, mums, or other garden flowers accented with silk or dried baby's breath and satin ribbon.

4. *What is the style and color of the Bride's gown?*
If the Bride's gown is white, you'll want to choose white flowers and white accents (pearls, tulle, lace, ribbon, etc.) for your bouquet. Similarly, if your gown is ivory, choose ivory flowers and accents. If you have a tailored, formal gown, a free-form or hand-wrapped bouquet with formal flowers may be the best choice. If you have chosen a formal, flowing, and elaborate gown, a formal cascade bouquet is in order. Round or oval bouquets are very versatile and can be used with many styles of gowns.

5. *What style and color(s) will the Attendants wear?*
The Attendants' attire should complement the Bride's gown style. Styles for the Bride and the Attendants vary from casual to very formal. Keep the style in mind when choosing your Attendants' bouquets. Color is a personal choice. Choose a color for their gowns that both you and your bridegroom like. Choosing A Color Scheme, pg. 3, can help you choose flower colors once the color for the attire is decided. Also consider whether or not you would like the Attendants to wear hats or hair accessories. If so, consider their differing hair styles when choosing a hat or hair accessory design.

6. *Where will the reception be held?*
For an outdoor reception, you may opt for casual flowers and simple table decorations. Consider that it may bc brcczy; you won't want your floral arrangements tipping over. The size of a reception hall or church hall may also determine how many and how large the floral designs can be. Attendants' bouquets may also be laid on the tables as decorations.

7. *How many corsages and boutonnieres will you need?*
Refer to the Wedding Flower Planning Guide, pg. 12, for suggestions of people you may wish to remember with a corsage or boutonniere.

CHOOSING A COLOR SCHEME

The color of the Attendants' gowns dictates the color scheme for the wedding and reception. The gowns and flowers work together to carry out the scheme, with the gowns becoming the background for the bouquets. We've included a color wheel to help you choose your floral colors.

When choosing colors for your wedding, don't be afraid of using color. The flowers don't have to be the same color as the gowns. Complementary and contrasting colors will show up nicely in your wedding photographs. To choose colors for your flowers, take a swatch of the gown fabric and find it on the color wheel. You probably won't be able to match it exactly, but find the basic hue. Now look at that color in relation to other colors on the wheel. Here are some traditional and attractive color combinations:

> **MONOCHROMATIC** — the subtle use of one color, with shades both lighter and darker.
>
> **COMPLEMENTARY** — the use of opposites on the color wheel.
>
> **ANALOGOUS** — the use of colors adjacent to each other on the color wheel within a 90° angle.
>
> **TRIADIC** — the use of three colors equidistant on the color wheel.

Remember that you don't have to use a color at its full intensity; a lighter or darker, muted version of hue may be more attractive. Whatever the colors ultimately selected, the flowers should always be accented with green foliage and other background materials.

When using ribbons or tulle in a bouquet, select a coordinating color or one that is somewhat lighter than the dominant color. Bows, streamers, ribbon loops, lace fans, tulle puffs, and pearl accents are used to complement the flowers and should not overpower the beauty of the flowers.

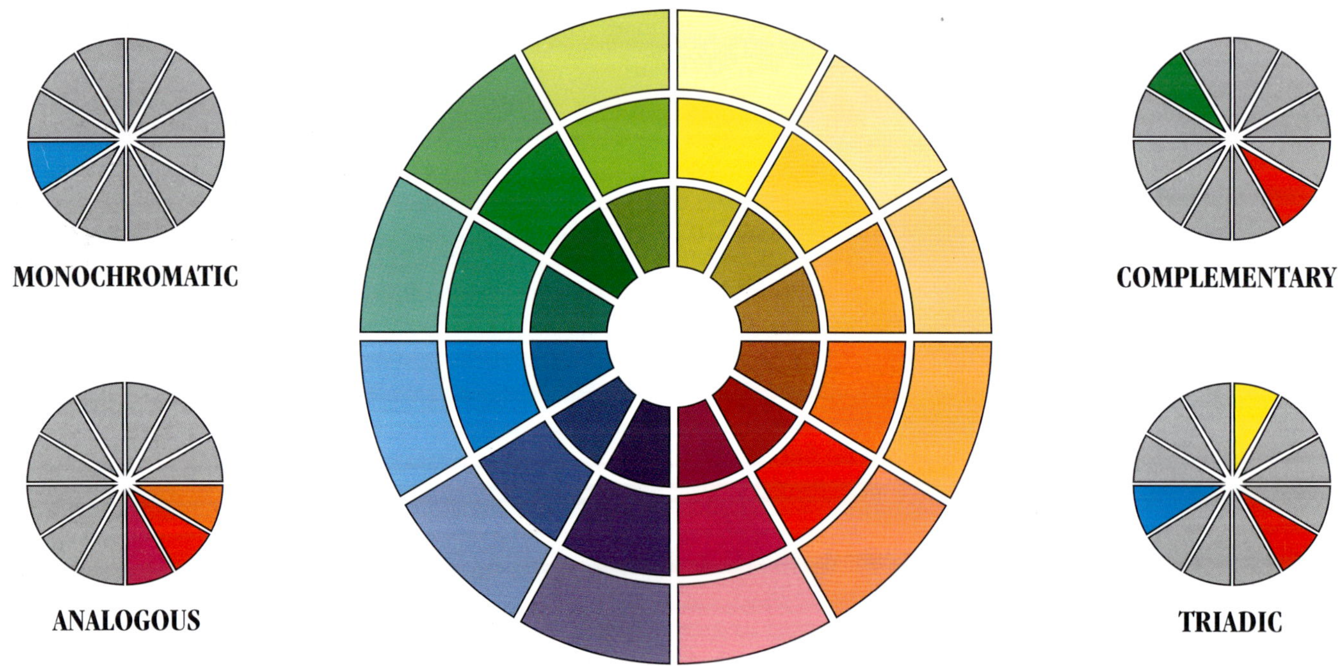

CHOOSING THE RIGHT BOUQUET

The style and color of the Bride's gown sets the tone for her bouquet. Whether her choice of gown is full length, tea length, or street length, her bouquet should complement its overall styling.

The Bride's bouquet has special distinction from all the others in the wedding party. Although the style and color of the gown are the first considerations, another factor governing the Bride's choice of bouquet style may be her height. For the tall Bride the bouquet may be larger and have long flowing lines or it may be more fully rounded in shape. Conversely, for the more petite Bride a smaller bouquet may look more in proportion. Whatever the ultimate choice of style, the bouquet should complement the beauty of the Bride and accentuate the loveliness of her gown — the bouquet should never overpower them.

Generally, the Attendants' bouquets are smaller and can be similar in design to that of the Bride. Flowers for the Matron or Maid of Honor can be different in color from the other Attendants', or the bouquet may be somewhat larger or have slightly different flowers. When planning bouquet styles for the Attendants, their height and general stature can help with the selection of the bouquet style. Just as with the tall Bride, tall Attendants can carry larger bouquets.

CHOOSING YOUR MATERIALS

Once you have considered all aspects of the wedding and the color scheme has been determined, make your floral selections to carry out the color scheme for the floral designs. Use the Wedding Flower Planning Guide, pg. 12, to write in the specific details for flowers needed.

BASIC FLORAL MATERIALS

With the selected design and a color scheme in mind, you are ready to choose your florals. Choose your FOCAL materials and LINE materials at the same time. While the FOCAL element is the most obvious part of the design, the LINE materials determine the shape and size of the design. The two should work together to create a lovely design. Choose SECONDARY materials to help control the light and dark aspects of the design. Finally, select the FILLER to blend, complement, and fill in the spaces of the finished design. Although most floral designs use the basic elements of FOCAL, LINE, SECONDARY, and FILLER materials, there are times when not all elements will be necessary.

When purchasing your flowers and greenery, you will find a wide variety available. In each materials list, we give you the total number of blossoms and/or leaves required for the floral design. You may be able to purchase one stem with the required number of blossoms or you may need to purchase several stems to have enough blossoms or leaves. For example, in the Love Is In The Air bouquet, pg. 15, you need 37 azalea blossoms. You could purchase a bush with 37 (or more) azaleas, six stems with seven azalea blossoms each, or 37 single azalea blossoms. Be sure to purchase all materials needed to complete the selected wedding floral designs plus a few extras. If a few more flowers or materials are needed at a later date, it may be difficult to find an exact match.

The basic and most versatile materials are:

Silk Flowers — The varieties, styles, colors, and sizes are endless — from the large, elegant blossoms used as FOCAL flowers, to the wispy, delicate sprays of tiny blossoms used in clusters for FILLER. Most silk flower stems also have silk leaves that may be removed and stemmed separately for FILLER. Although referred to as "silk" flowers, most are made from silk-like materials. Quality and prices vary. Select the best quality possible for your wedding designs. (***Note:*** *Rosebuds, used extensively in wedding designs, are available in at least 4 sizes. The Rosebuds in this book are identified as large (2"), medium (1½"), small (1"), and mini (½"-¾") and are measured from top of bud to calyx.)*

Wedding Sprays and Flowers — These flowers, specifically designed for weddings, are made of nylon, satin, or other sheer materials and may be referred to as "sheers". Some even have pearl accents. Available in white, ivory, and many other colors, these wedding sprays and flowers add an elegant touch to bouquets, corsages, and hair accessories.

Greenery — Stems of ornamental leaves, ferns, and plants are often used to establish the LINE or as FILLER. Ornamental leaves may create the LINE in hand-wrapped designs. Greenery bushes are available in many styles and colors and provide many leaves. Always save extra leaves to be stemmed and used separately as fillers.

Naturals — Many types of preserved materials are available in a wide variety of colors and textures. Small blossoms are used as FILLER. Among the favorites used in wedding designs are preserved ferns and dried baby's breath. These add soft accents and are used to fill in spaces among flowers and leaves.

Bouquet Holder — Several types of holders are available with top surface diameters ranging from 2½" to 4½". Bouquets in this book use a 4" diameter holder although the 3" and 4½" are also suitable. (*Note: The smaller 2½" size was used only for the Throw Bouquet on pg. 47.*) Holders come with various foam materials firmly attached to their plastic bases. Those designed specifically for silk and dried or preserved materials are used when stems are relatively short and/or slender. When stems are thicker and/or longer, a firm plastic foam (Styrofoam™) base bouquet holder is best. All Bridal and Attendant bouquets in this book requiring a bouquet holder are designed so that they are carried in the palm of the hand with the handle pointed **downward**.

Lace Collar — Several sizes of collars, available in white or ivory, are made to slip onto the handle of the bouquet holders, giving a delicate outline to bouquets. After slipping the collar onto the holder, hot glue the inside of the collar to the outside of the holder. Also, cut off the plastic prongs that extend from the hole in the collar. (*Note: Do not cut off prongs when assembling the Rose Cluster Bouquet on pg. 60.*)

Floral Wire — A lightweight, flexible wire of 24-30 gauge is used where a heavier, stiffer wire may not be appropriate. Cloth-covered floral wire is recommended to secure bows, ribbon loops, lace fans, and tulle puffs. (*Note: The higher the gauge number, the finer the wire.*)

Stem Wire — 16-22 gauge wire lengths are used for adding new stems or for lengthening or strengthening original stems.

Floral Pick — A small wood pick that has a thin wire attached to one end provides a sturdy stem for some florals.

Floral Tape — This paper tape becomes sticky when stretched. Use floral tape to wrap several stems together into a single stem, to secure a wire to lengthen or strengthen an existing stem, or to attach wire to replace an original stem.

Ribbon — Satin, lace, or acetate ribbons are used to make bows, streamers, ribbon loops, and fans. Common ribbon sizes are listed below.

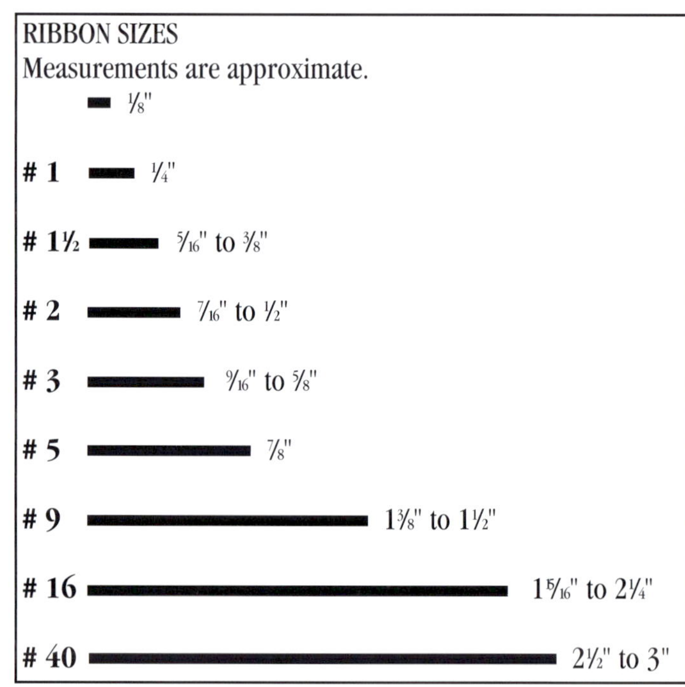

RIBBON SIZES	
Measurements are approximate.	
	⅛"
# 1	¼"
# 1½	⁵⁄₁₆" to ⅜"
# 2	⁷⁄₁₆" to ½"
# 3	⁹⁄₁₆" to ⅝"
# 5	⅞"
# 9	1⅜" to 1½"
# 16	1⁵⁄₁₆" to 2¼"
# 40	2½" to 3"

Decorative Cording and Tubing — These products are used for bows and accents in some designs.

Along with these basic floral supplies, **wire cutters**, **scissors**, a **glue gun**, **glue sticks**, and a **ruler** are also essential.

PREPARATION

Now that you have purchased all your necessary materials, you're ready to prepare them for assembly.

PREPARING THE FLORALS

The first step in preparing most of the florals is to remove the leaves. This will allow you to easily position each blossom as indicated in the placement diagram or photo. Leaves and small blossoms may be used singly, as sprigs, or in clusters. You may wish to add a dot or line of glue on backside of each leaf or flower petal along the plastic veins or wires for reinforcement.

The decision to "stem" a flower, leaf, or other material largely depends upon where the stem will be placed and/or how the stem will ultimately be used in the design. Quite often original stems need to be lengthened or strengthened, and sometimes stems need to be replaced to give a more flexible, pliable stem. Also, when an original stem contains no wire to support it, a stem wire should be added.

All new stems should be wrapped with floral tape. To use floral tape, stretch and fold tape around stem directly below flower or leaf. Roll stem into the tape while gently stretching it downward, forming a tight spiral around stem. Overlapping tape edges, continue wrapping to stem end. Tear off excess tape; wind tape around bottom of stem.

The portion of stem or wire to be inserted into a foam base or holder should always be wrapped with floral tape to ensure that the materials remain firmly in place.

The stemming method used often depends upon the construction of the flower and the manner in which it is attached to its original stem. Choose from the following techniques the method best suited for the particular flower or leaf being used.

•**Side-by-Side Method** — This method lengthens, strengthens, or replaces the original stem. Place stem wire alongside original stem and wrap with floral tape around entire length needed.

To add new stem   To lengthen or strengthen stem

•**Piercing Method** — This method is the most effective way to secure a flower with a plastic calyx to a new stem. **Exercise caution when using hot wire.** Heat end of bare stem wire for a few seconds in a candle flame and carefully poke heated end through calyx from side to side. When end of wire is cool, bring it down to meet other end below calyx and tape together. If a stronger stem is needed, add another stem wire alongside the piercing wire.

•**Hook Method** — This method gives a firm stem to a sprig, cluster, or spray. Hook end of stem wire over lowest stem. Bring wire ends together and wrap wire and stem with floral tape.

•**Floral Pick Method** — To lengthen or strengthen a stem, add a floral pick. Lay stem alongside pick, wrap wire around stem and pick, then wrap with floral tape.

PREPARING THE FILLERS

Flowers and dried or preserved materials that are being used as fillers should be prepared in the same manner as other florals. Here are some tips for preparing other FILLER materials.

Keep FILLER materials rather short, not allowing them to extend beyond the length of other flowers in the design.

The wire used to secure center of bows or to hold ribbon loops must be long enough to form a stem to be inserted into bouquet holder or to be added to a corsage or other design.

•**Making Ribbon, Cording, Tubing, or Lace Loops** — Form loop; gather and wrap ends with cloth-covered floral wire. Add stem wire and wrap with floral tape. Loops may be made individually, doubled, or in multiple groups.

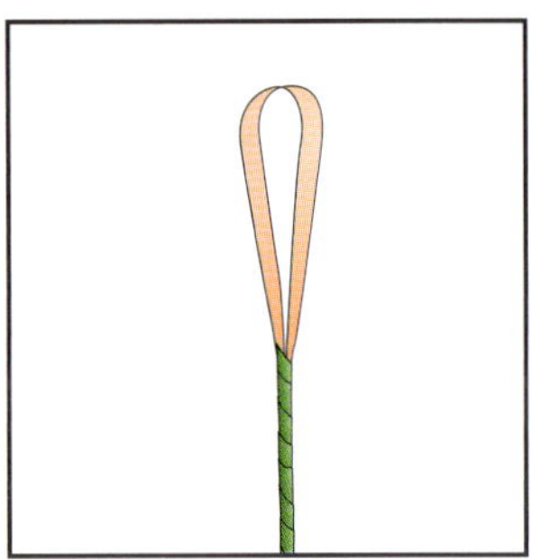
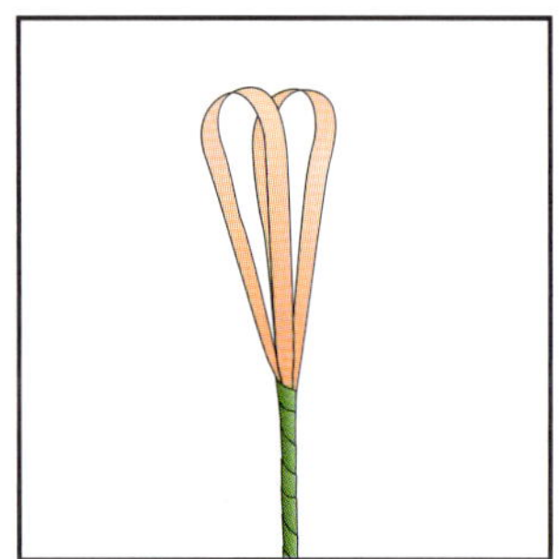

•**Making Lace Fans** — Accordion pleat a 6"-12" length of lace and staple at one end to secure. Run floral wire through bottom edge; wrap with floral tape. Use stem wire instead if the fan is to be inserted into a foam base.

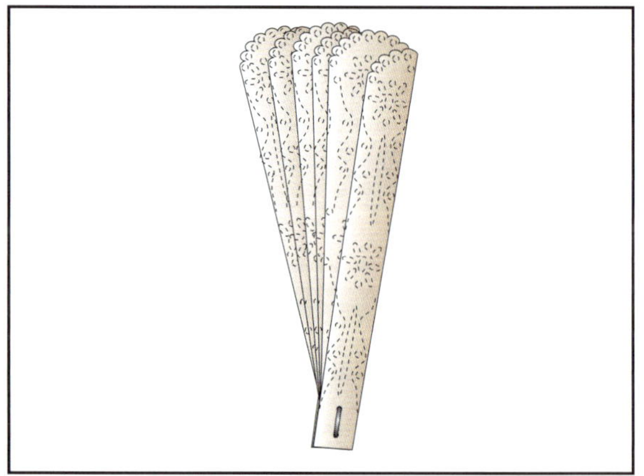

•**Making Tulle Puffs** — Use a 6" square of tulle for each puff. Use whichever assembly option you prefer.

Option A — Bring corners of square together; insert floral wire through tulle ½" from held point. Tightly wrap wire around tulle. Add stem wire and wrap with floral tape.

Option B — Hold at center of square; insert floral wire through tulle ½" from held point. Tightly wrap wire around tulle. Add stem wire and wrap with floral tape.

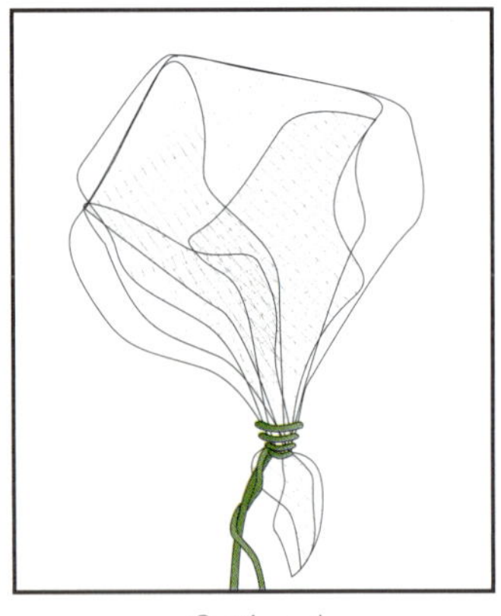

Option A   Option B

ASSEMBLY TECHNIQUES

With the wedding floral design chosen, the flowers and materials selected, and the tools and supplies gathered, the assembly is ready to begin!

ASSEMBLY TIPS

• Separate flowers and greenery into groups of FOCAL, LINE, SECONDARY, and FILLER as appropriate for the selected floral design.

• Apply hot glue to each wrapped stem before inserting the stem approximately 1" into foam base.

• For ease in assembling bouquet in a holder, place handle with lace collar into the neck of a tall, wide-based, empty glass bottle; position handle at the proper angle for inserting flowers and other materials.

• While assembling most bouquets, keep the face of a clock in mind. This helps to keep the bouquet balanced and symmetrical. For example, if a flower is placed at 2 o'clock, a matching flower should also be placed at 8 o'clock.

• When wrapping more than three or four stems together, as in a hand-wrapped bouquet, corsage, or similar design, cut stems to varying lengths below the tape point before the final wrapping to avoid a bulky, unattractive bundle of stems.

• When duplicating two or more Attendants' bouquets, work in an assembly line procedure instead of completing one at a time. By inserting one group of materials at a time into each holder, the finished bouquets will be identical.

• To curve stems of silk flowers and greenery, exert slight pressure on wire stem. If the stem does not bend, hold it in hot water to soften the plastic coating.

• Save any wire cut from flowers or leaf sprays to be used to stem other short flowers, leaves, and fillers.

• Save extra leaves to be used as fillers.

• For a special finishing touch, add a few tiny blossoms, leaves, or a small bow on the backside of bouquet holder where the handle comes through the lace collar.

• Floral scents are available to add a pleasing aroma to silk floral designs.

• When your bouquet is completed, you may find that a stem is too long. To shorten the stem, carefully remove flower head from stem, then cut top of stem; replace and hot glue flower head in place. If, due to wiring of the flower head, the stem must be removed from foam to shorten it, re-tape entire stem length or add floral tape to the portion to be re-inserted into foam.

• For added protection and stability, lightly spray finished design with matte finish clear acrylic sealer. This will keep any dried or preserved materials from shedding.

• If bouquet is saved after the wedding, periodically blow any dust away with a hand-held hair dryer on low setting.

METHODS OF ASSEMBLY

Most designs are made simply by inserting stems into a foam base, but the following methods are also used.

• **Corsage method** — The corsage method is used to assemble small, compact groupings of flowers and greenery to make corsages, boutonnieres, and hair accessories. These designs usually contain FOCAL, SECONDARY, and FILLER materials. The assembly begins with one or more FOCAL flowers held in one hand. The other materials are nestled at varying heights around the FOCAL flower and floral taped one at a time to the main stem. When all stems are secured, trim them at varying lengths to avoid a bulky stem. A bow may be taped under the lowest flower. Trim stems to 3" or less and wrap entire length with floral tape.

•**Hand-Wrap Method** — Emphasize the line and beauty of the materials being used with the hand-wrap method rather than establishing a well-defined pattern as in other designs. Large flowers on long stems may be incorporated into the design with all stems secured at a single tape point.

Starting with stem of FOCAL flower held in one hand, add another stem alongside the first by wrapping floral tape one time around these two stems at the tape point. Add another stem to other side of first stem in the same manner, wrapping one time around it to join the three stems at the tape point. Continue until all the greenery, flowers, and filler materials are joined at the tape point.

Below tape point, stems must be cut to varying lengths to assure a tapered handle. After stems are cut, securely wrap entire handle with floral tape.

•**Cascade Method** — Long hanging groups of flowers and leaves or a continuous garland of flowers and leaves can be formed with the cascade method. Each component is floral taped one at a time to main stem, forming a repeating pattern along stem.

•**Cluster Method** — Group two or more sprigs, leaves, or flowers together to form a cluster and then wrap with floral tape to create a single stem.

WEDDING FLOWER PLANNING GUIDE

Wedding Date ____ Location _____________________________

BRIDE   height __________ size __________

Gown color _________________________ Style ____________

Bouquet Style ______________________________________

Headpiece ____

Garter ____

Throw Bouquet ______________________________________

Going-Away Corsage __________________________________

Flowers & Supplies __________________________________

____

____

____

____

____

____

____

ATTENDANTS — Maid of Honor, Bridesmaids

Name	Hgt.	Size	Gown Color and Style
____	____	____	____________________
____	____	____	____________________
____	____	____	____________________
____	____	____	____________________
____	____	____	____________________

Bouquet Style ______________________________________

____

Hair Accessories ____________________________________

____

Flowers & Supplies __________________________________

____

____

____

____

____

____

____

____

____

____

____

____

____

____

____

FLOWER GIRL   height __________ size __________ age ______

Gown color _________________ Bouquet Style ___________

Hair Accessory _____________________________________

Flowers & Supplies __________________________________

____

____

BOUTONNIERES   how many __________

Groom   height __________

Groomsmen/Ushers ___________________________________

____

Fathers ____

____

Grandfathers _______________________________________

____

Others (Clergyman, Musician, etc.) ___________________

____

Flowers & Supplies __________________________________

____

____

RING BEARER   height __________ age __________

Pillow ____

Boutonniere ____

Flowers & Supplies __________________________________

____

____

CORSAGES   how many __________

Mothers (Pin-On or Wristlet) _________________________

____

Grandmothers ______________________________________

____

Others (Musicians, Servers, etc.) ____________________

____

____

Flowers & Supplies __________________________________

____

____

ALTAR/PEW BOWS

____

____

Flowers & Supplies __________________________________

____

____

RECEPTION   location _______________________________

Cake Table ____

____

____

Guest Tables — how many ____________________________

____

Flowers & Supplies __________________________________

____

____

ROMANTIC INTERLUDE

Approximate size: 13" wide x 18" long

This natural-looking Bride's oval bouquet gives you the perfect opportunity to mix different types of flowers. This bouquet can also be accented with delicate fillers, ribbon or lace loops, or bows for softness. This style may be transformed into a heart shape by tucking down the center top edge of the lace collar and at the same time slightly shortening the stem length of the flowers at the 12 o'clock position. The style of this bouquet is appropriate for both Bride's and Attendants' bouquets.

Familiarize yourself with the information found on pgs. 2-11. Stem lengths indicated are measured from the TOP of blossom, leaf, or preserved material and include 1" to be inserted into foam base.

MATERIALS

Bouquet holder; 9" lace collar; **FOCAL:** 5 lilies; **SECONDARY:** 16 sweet pea blossoms; **LINE:** 8 orchid sprays with 4 blossoms each; **FILLER:** 4 lily buds, dried baby's breath, 48 sprigs of mini philodendron leaves, 36 sprigs of parsley leaves, 12 pearl sprays; 2 yds of 4mm string pearls.

ASSEMBLY INSTRUCTIONS

1. Place holder into lace collar.
2. Remove stamens from lilies. Glue a pearl spray in center of each lily, trimming pearl spray stem as necessary.
3. Prepare and stem materials, referring to diagrams and as follows:
   - Lilies — five $5\frac{1}{2}$"
   - Lily buds — one 5", two 6", and one 8"
   - Baby's breath clusters (3 sprigs each) — eight 4", fourteen $4\frac{1}{2}$", two 5", and two $5\frac{1}{2}$"
   - Parsley leaf clusters (3 sprigs each) — twelve $3\frac{1}{2}$"
   - Philodendron clusters (3 sprigs each) — twelve $4\frac{1}{2}$", two 8", and two 9"
   - Pearl sprays — seven $5\frac{1}{2}$"
4. Insert lilies, sweet peas, and orchid sprays, referring to diagrams for placement. While assembling this bouquet, keep the face of a clock in mind.
5. Insert clusters of philodendron and parsley leaves around flowers, placing longer philodendron clusters on the sides near the bottom and curving them toward the center.
6. Insert baby's breath clusters and lily buds, placing longer lily buds at the bottom.
7. Accent with pearl sprays.
8. Cut a 21", a 23", and a 25" length of string pearls. Stem each end of each length of pearls and insert into sides of bouquet.

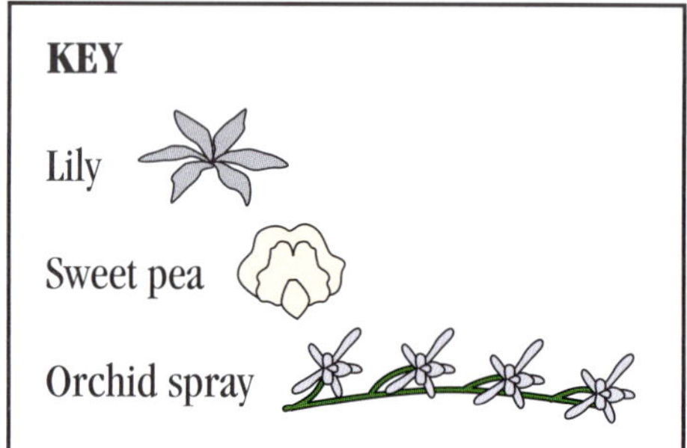

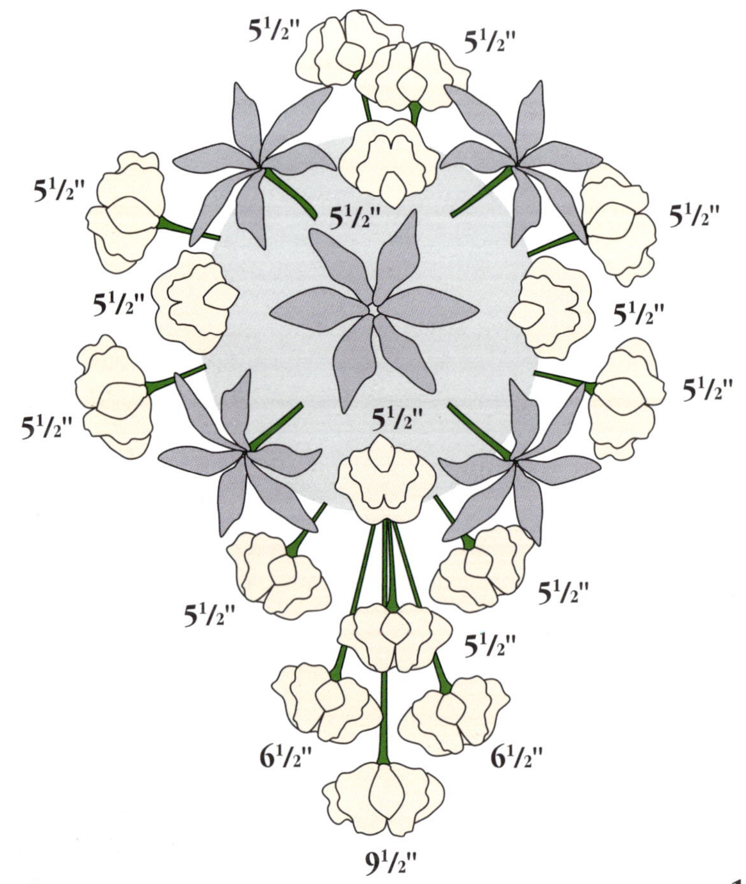

ROMANTIC INTERLUDE BRIDAL BOUQUET

LOVE IS IN THE AIR

Approximate size: 12" round

This round Bridal bouquet is considered an "all-purpose" style because almost any size and shape flower can be used to create the basic shape. The rounded line can be made larger or smaller if desired and any attractive lace or ribbon may be used for accent.

Familiarize yourself with the information found on pgs. 2-11. Stem lengths indicated are measured from the TOP of blossom, leaf, or preserved material and include 1" to be inserted into foam base.

MATERIALS

Bouquet holder; 9" lace collar; **FOCAL:** 9 roses; **SECONDARY:** 37 azalea blossoms with leaves; **FILLER:** 92 sprigs of silk baby's breath, 50-80 rose leaves; 2¼ yds of #9 ribbon.

ASSEMBLY INSTRUCTIONS

1. Place holder into lace collar.
2. Set aside 2 azalea blossoms and 2 sprigs of baby's breath.
3. Prepare and stem materials, referring to diagram and as follows:

   Azaleas — twenty-three 6" and twelve 5"
   Baby's breath clusters (3 sprigs each) — thirty 4½"
   Rose leaf clusters (3-6 leaves each) — fourteen 4½"

4. Insert roses and azaleas, referring to diagrams for placement and placing longer azalea stems around the outer edges and shorter stems in the center.
5. Insert clusters of baby's breath and rose leaves around flowers.
6. Cut a 13", a 16", and an 18" length of ribbon. Make into one multiple loop and insert into bouquet.
7. Cut an 8", a 9", and a 13" length of ribbon for streamers. Place lengths together and stem one end. Glue remaining azalea and baby's breath blossoms to longest streamer. Insert into bouquet.

LOVE IS IN THE AIR BRIDAL BOUQUET

ELEGANCE IN WHITE

Approximate size: 12" wide x 17" long

This Bridal bouquet is truly classic in its traditionally elegant styling. Its flattering lines especially complement a full-skirted gown. The length of the cascade flowing from the bottom of the bouquet should be made in proportion to the height of the person carrying it — the taller the person, the longer the cascade may be.

Familiarize yourself with the information found on pgs. 2-11. Stem lengths indicated are measured from the TOP of blossom, leaf, or preserved material and include 1" to be inserted into foam base.

MATERIALS

Bouquet holder; 9" lace collar; **FOCAL:** 7 carnations; **SECONDARY:** 12 large rosebuds; **FILLER:** 74 sprigs of silk baby's breath, 17 pearl sprays with 2 pearls each, 60-90 rose leaves, preserved plumosus fern, 72 sprigs of parsley leaves; 1³/₄ yds of decorative cording.

ASSEMBLY INSTRUCTIONS

1. Place holder into lace collar.
2. Prepare and stem materials, referring to diagrams and as follows:

    Baby's breath clusters (2 sprigs each)— thirty-seven 4"
    Plumosus fern clusters (7 sprigs each)— nine 5"
    Parsley leaf clusters (6 sprigs each)— twelve 3¹/₂"
    Pearl sprays — seventeen 4¹/₂"
    Cascade — 5 baby's breath clusters, 1 carnation, 2 parsley leaf clusters, 3 plumosus fern clusters, 3 pearl sprays, and 6 rose leaves to make a 10" long cascade
    Rose leaf clusters (3-5 leaves each) — fifteen 5¹/₂"

3. Insert carnations, rosebuds, and cascade, referring to diagrams for placement.
4. Insert parsley leaf clusters and rose leaves around flowers.
5. Accent with baby's breath clusters, pearl sprays, and plumosus fern clusters.
6. Cut five 8" lengths of cording. Make into 5 loops; insert into bouquet. Cut a 21" length of cording. Stem each end of cording and insert into sides of bouquet.

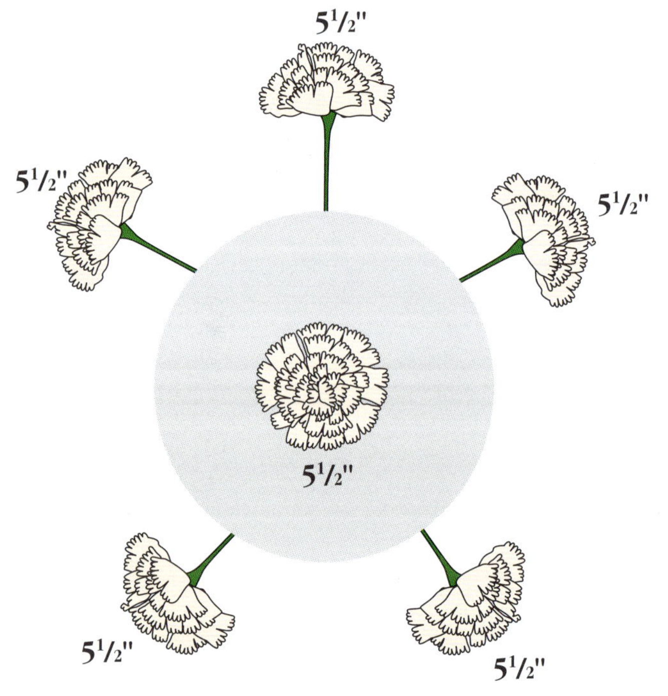

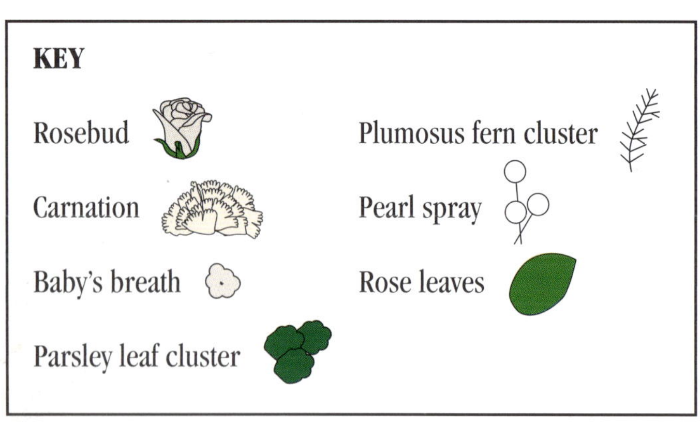

ELEGANCE IN WHITE BRIDAL BOUQUET

LOVE IN THE MIST

Approximate size: 14" wide x 14" long

Natural…airy…flowing…movement — all define this free-form Bridal style. It is important to remember that even in free-form designing, a basic shape must be maintained. Once the shape is established, position the flowers in the direction they would naturally grow, keeping softness and airiness in mind.

Familiarize yourself with the information found on pgs. 2-11. Stem lengths indicated are measured from the TOP of blossom, leaf, or preserved material and include 1" to be inserted into foam base.

MATERIALS

Bouquet holder; 9" lace collar; **FOCAL:** 9 large rosebuds; **SECONDARY:** 17 lilac spikes; **LINE:** 26 Boston fern fronds; **FILLER:** 80 rose leaves, 6 lilac blossoms, preserved plumosus fern, 1⅓ yds of 6"w tulle; 1¼ yds of #3 ribbon.

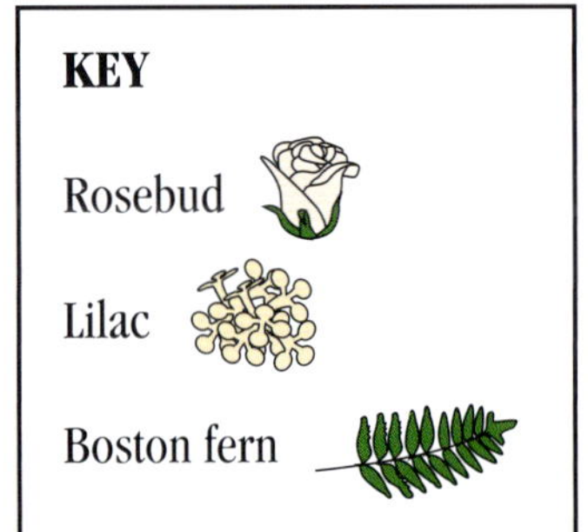

ASSEMBLY INSTRUCTIONS

1. Place holder into lace collar.
2. Cut one 13" and two 12" lengths of ribbon. Glue 2 lilac blossoms to one end of each length. Stem each ribbon length.
3. Prepare and stem materials, referring to diagram and as follows:

   Rosebuds — nine 6"
   Lilac spikes — sixteen 6" and one 9"
   Plumosus fern clusters (7 sprigs each)— twenty 6"
   Tulle puffs — 8 with 2½" stems
   Rose leaf clusters (5 leaves each) — sixteen 4"
4. Insert Boston fern, rosebuds, and lilacs, referring to diagrams for placement and placing longest lilac at bottom of bouquet.
5. Insert plumosus fern clusters and rose leaf clusters around flowers.
6. Accent with tulle puffs.
7. Insert ribbon lengths into bottom of bouquet.

LOVE IN THE MIST BRIDAL BOUQUET

LOVELY LILIES

Approximate size: 16" wide x 27" long

The simplicity of the line along with the elegance of the flowers used makes a striking Bridal bouquet. This hand-wrapped style requires only a few flowers and provides an excellent opportunity to incorporate some unusual FOCAL flowers. Pick large flowers with sturdy stems for FOCAL flowers. The stems serve as the handle for this easy-to-make bouquet.

Familiarize yourself with the information found on pgs. 2-11. Stem lengths indicated are measured from the TOP of blossom, leaf, or preserved material.

MATERIALS

FOCAL: 8 calla lilies; **LINE:** 7 orchid stems with multiple blossoms on each; **FILLER:** 4 stems of huckleberry leaves; 3 yds of #9 ribbon; 2¼ yds of 6"w tulle.

ASSEMBLY INSTRUCTIONS

1. Prepare and stem materials, referring to diagrams and as follows:

    Huckleberry — one 16", one 18", one 21", and one 24"

2. The 27" calla lily is the main stem. Add the other calla lilies to the main stem, taping at the tape point and referring to diagram for placement. Bend stems as desired.

3. Tape orchid stems to main stem, referring to diagram for placement. Bend stems as desired.

4. Tape huckleberry stems to main stem, taping at the tape point. Bend stems as desired.

5. Cut a 64" length of ribbon for bow; set aside.

6. To create the handle, start at tape point and wrap the stems from top to bottom with remaining ribbon; glue.

7. Use 64" ribbon length to make an 8-loop bow with 3½" to 4" loops; glue bow to tape point.

8. Use tulle to make an 8-loop bow with 5" loops; glue to back of bouquet at tape point.

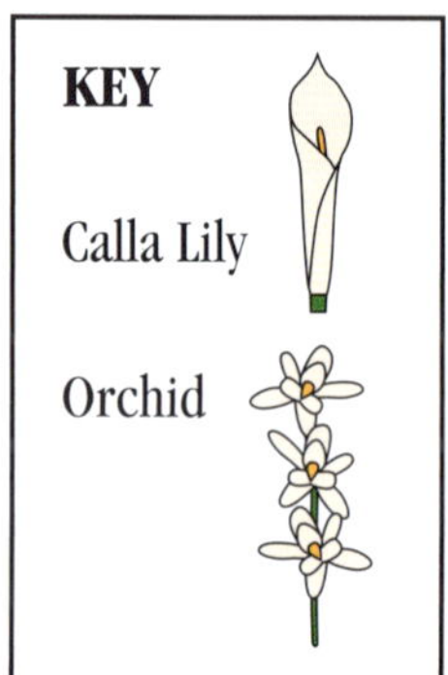

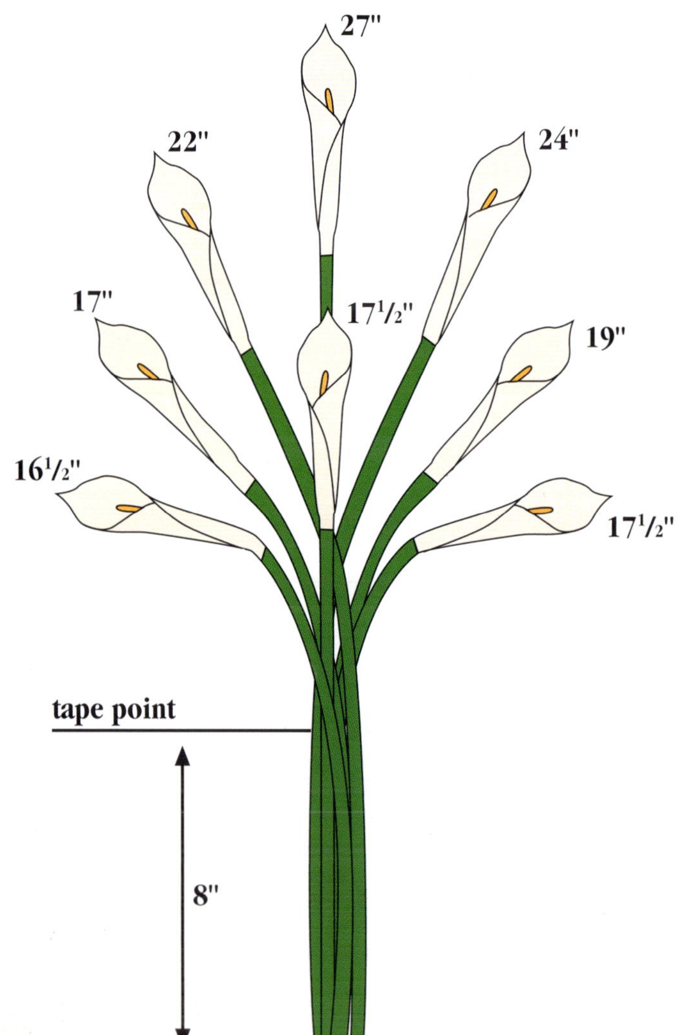

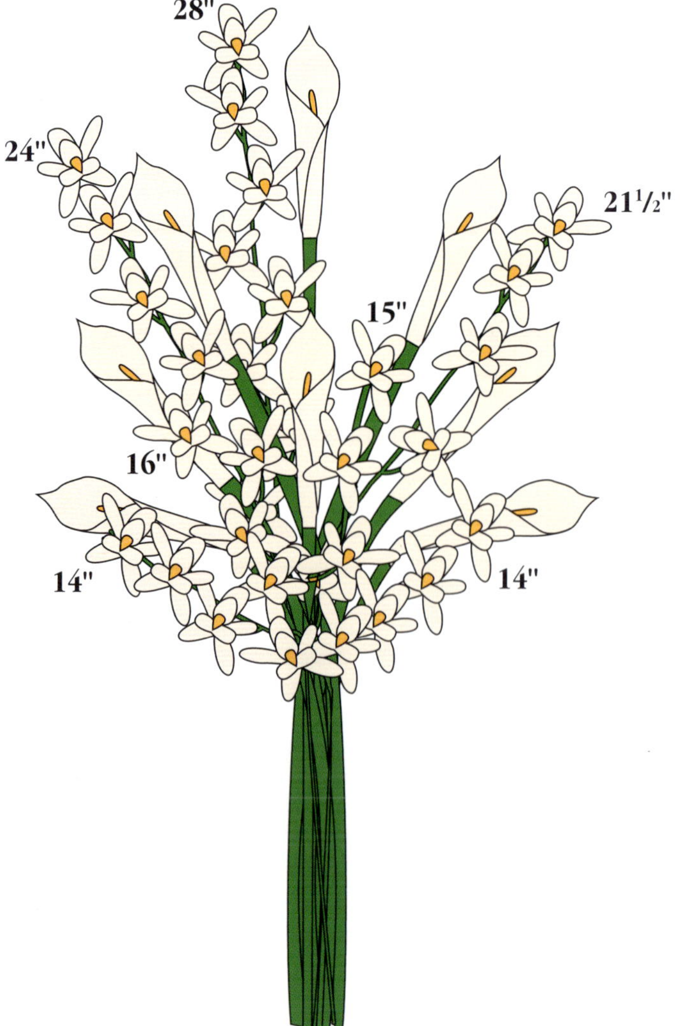

LOVELY LILIES BRIDAL BOUQUET

CAPTIVATING CHARM

Approximate size: 14¹/₂" wide x 20" long

This hand-wrapped Bridal bouquet can be completed with a minimum amount of materials and is one of the easiest bouquets to make. The finished bouquet can be casual or highly sophisticated depending upon the flowers and greenery chosen. With rather tall and relatively narrow lines, the materials are placed vertically or only slightly angled outward, avoiding any great emphasis on horizontal lines. This bouquet is carried with the stem in the palm of the hand, allowing the bouquet to rest gracefully in the bend of the elbow.

Familiarize yourself with the information found on pgs. 2-11. Stem lengths indicated are measured from the TOP of blossom, leaf, or preserved material.

MATERIALS

FOCAL: 10 roses; **SECONDARY:** 6 freesia stems with 3 blossoms each; **FILLER:** 5 liatris spikes, 4 stems of leatherleaf fern with 5 fronds each, preserved plumosus fern; 5¹/₂ yds of 6"w tulle; 2 yds of #5 lace ribbon.

ASSEMBLY INSTRUCTIONS

1. Prepare and stem materials, referring to diagrams and as follows:

    Liatris — one 12", three 15", and one 19"

    Leatherleaf fern — four 15¹/₂"

    Plumosus fern clusters (7 sprigs each) — two 12", one 15", and one 16"

2. The 20" rose is the main stem. Add the other roses to the main stem, taping at the tape point and referring to diagram for placement. Bend stems as desired.

3. Tape freesia stems to main stem, referring to diagram for placement. Bend stems as desired.
4. Tape liatris stems to main stem. Bend stems as desired.
5. Add leatherleaf fern stems to back of bouquet and tape to main stem.
6. Tape plumosus fern clusters to bouquet.
7. Cut a 4¹/₂ yd length of tulle for bow; set aside.
8. To create the handle, start at tape point and wrap the stems from top to bottom with remaining tulle; glue.
9. Use 4¹/₂ yd length of tulle to make a 16-loop bow with 5" loops; glue bow to top of tape point.
10. Cut five 13" lengths of lace ribbon. Glue each length to handle under bow. Trim ends as desired.

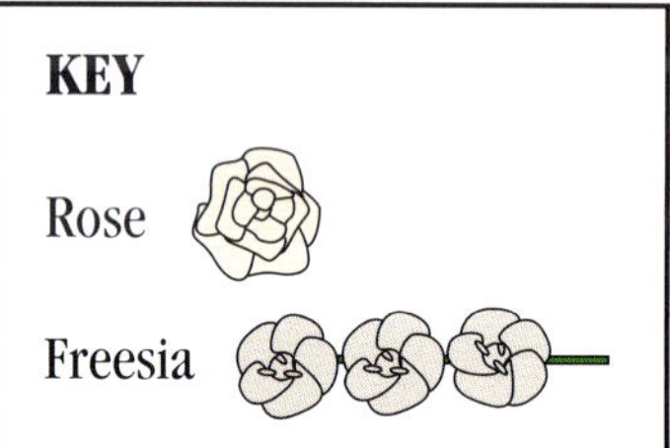

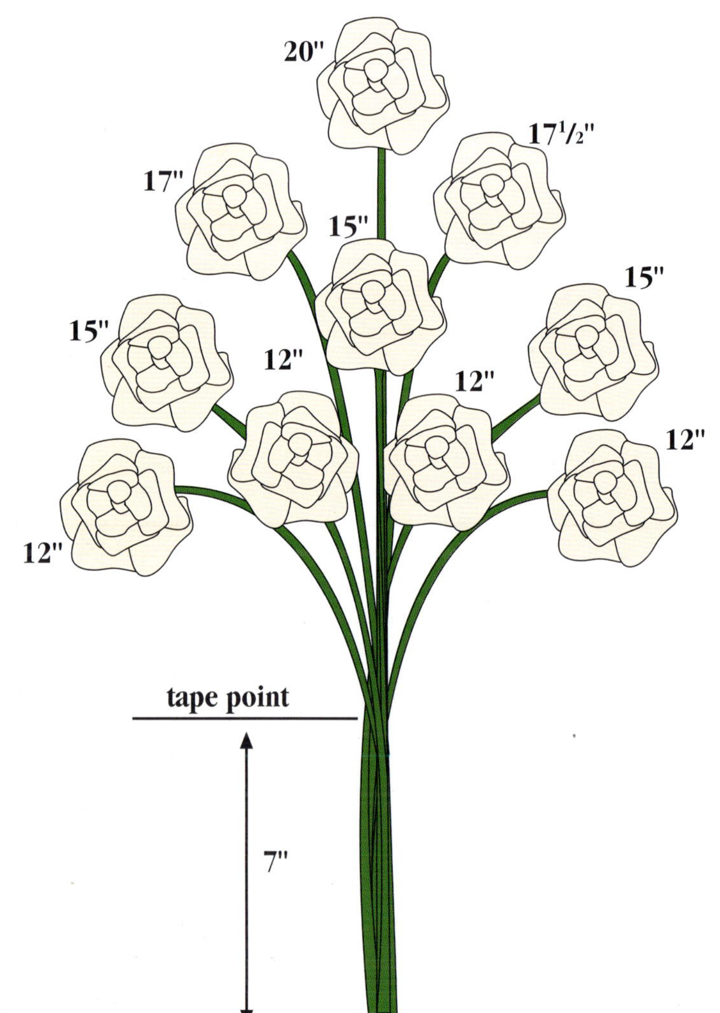

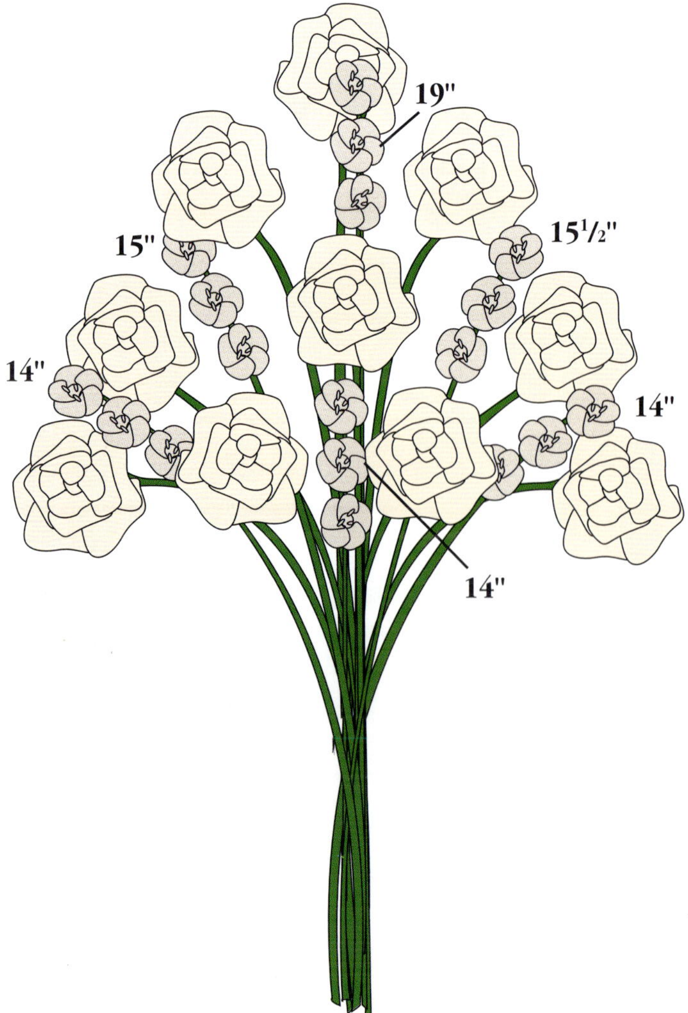

CAPTIVATING CHARM BRIDAL BOUQUET

MOONLIT EVENING

Approximate size: 12" wide x 19" long

The graceful elegance of this crescent-shaped Bridal bouquet is achieved through the placement of the curving cascade. Its pleasing, well-defined lines complement many gown styles.

Familiarize yourself with the information found on pgs. 2-11. Stem lengths indicated are measured from the TOP of blossom, leaf, or preserved material and include 1" to be inserted into foam base.

MATERIALS

Bouquet holder; 9" lace collar; **FOCAL:** 8 gardenias with leaves; **SECONDARY:** 14 stephanotis blossoms; **FILLER:** 13 pearl sprays, 67 sprigs of boxwood leaves; $^3/_4$ yd of 3"w lace.

ASSEMBLY INSTRUCTIONS

1. Place holder into lace collar.
2. Prepare and stem materials, referring to diagrams and as follows:

    Cascade — 3 boxwood leaf sprigs, 5 stephanotis blossoms, 2 pearl sprays, and 1 gardenia to make a $10^1/_2$" long cascade

    Boxwood leaf clusters (4 sprigs each) — sixteen $4^1/_2$"
    Pearl sprays — eleven 4"

3. Insert gardenias, stephanotis blossoms, and cascade, referring to diagrams for placement.
4. Insert boxwood leaf clusters around flowers.
5. Cut a 9" and an 11" length of lace for streamers; turn one cut edge of each length of lace to wrong side and glue in place. Stem cut end of each streamer. Insert streamers into bouquet near cascade; glue streamers to cascade as desired.
6. Accent bouquet and streamers with pearl sprays.
7. Make lace loop with remaining lace and insert into right side of bouquet.

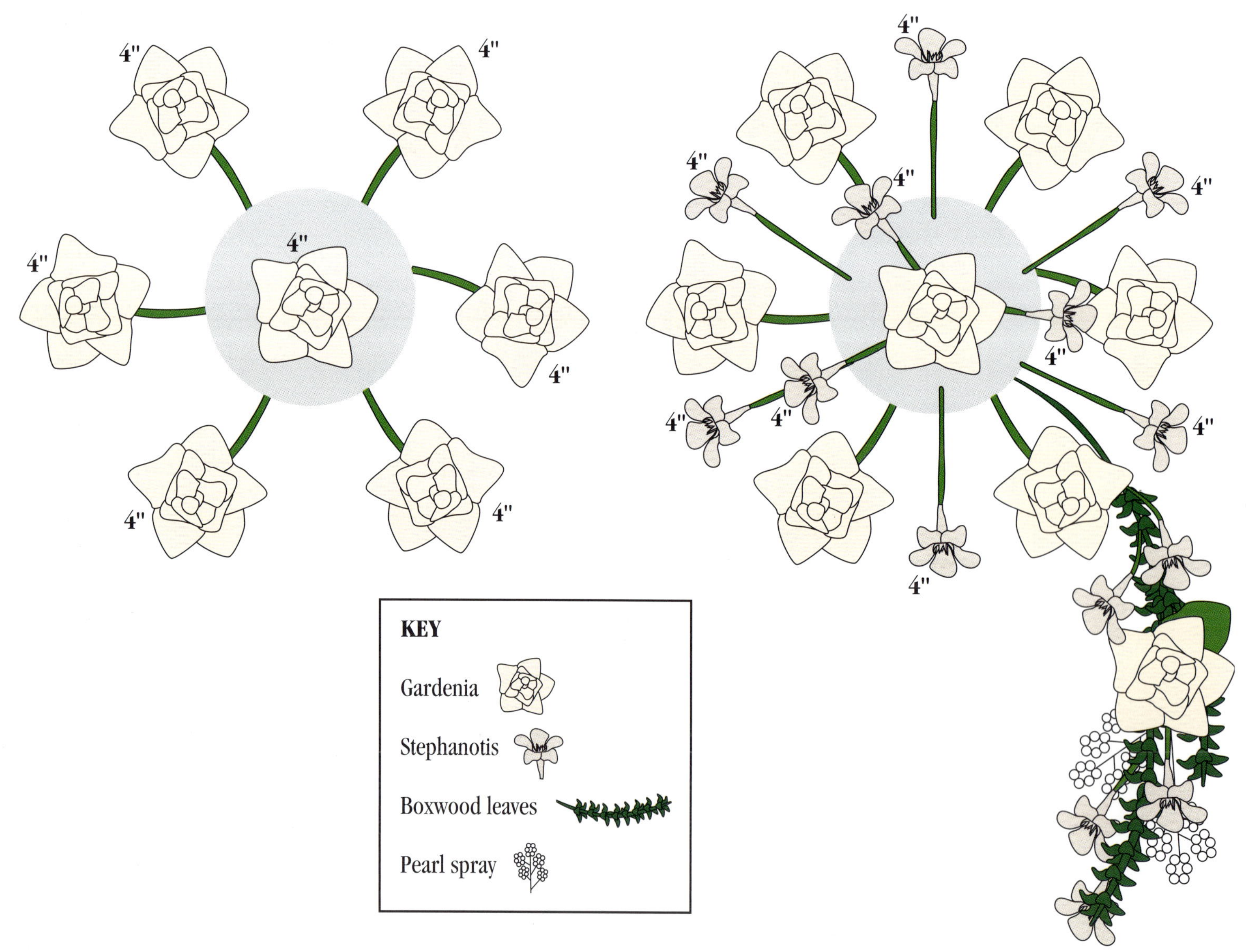

MOONLIT EVENING BRIDAL BOUQUET

SOPHISTICATE

Approximate size: 12" wide x 16" long

The construction techniques for this angular Attendant's style are very similar to those used to make round bouquets. The addition of lovely FOCAL flowers cascading at an angle across the bouquet give a special touch of elegance.

Familiarize yourself with the information found on pgs. 2-11. Stem lengths indicated are measured from the TOP of blossom, leaf, or preserved material and include 1" to be inserted into foam base.

MATERIALS

Bouquet holder; 8" lace collar; **FOCAL:** 5 roses; **SECONDARY:** 5 medium rosebuds, 13 morning glory blossoms; **FILLER:** 15 Boston fern fronds, 7 morning glory buds, 8 clusters of satin phlox, 9 sprigs of silk statice, preserved plumosus fern; 1 yd of #5 lace ribbon.

ASSEMBLY INSTRUCTIONS

1. Place holder into lace collar.
2. Prepare and stem materials, referring to diagrams and as follows:
   Boston fern fronds — thirteen 5½" and two 6"
   Morning glory buds — one 5", three 5½", one 6", one 7", and one 10"
   Phlox clusters — six 4" and two 4½"
   Statice sprigs — three 5½", five 6½", and one 7"

Plumosus fern clusters (7 sprigs each) — eight 5" and four 5½"

3. Insert roses, rosebuds, and morning glory blossoms, referring to diagrams for placement.
4. Insert morning glory buds, Boston fern fronds, and plumosus fern clusters, placing longer stems at the upper left and lower right.
5. Accent with phlox clusters and statice sprigs.
6. Cut ribbon into 3 equal lengths. Place lengths together and stem one end. Insert lengths in bottom of bouquet.

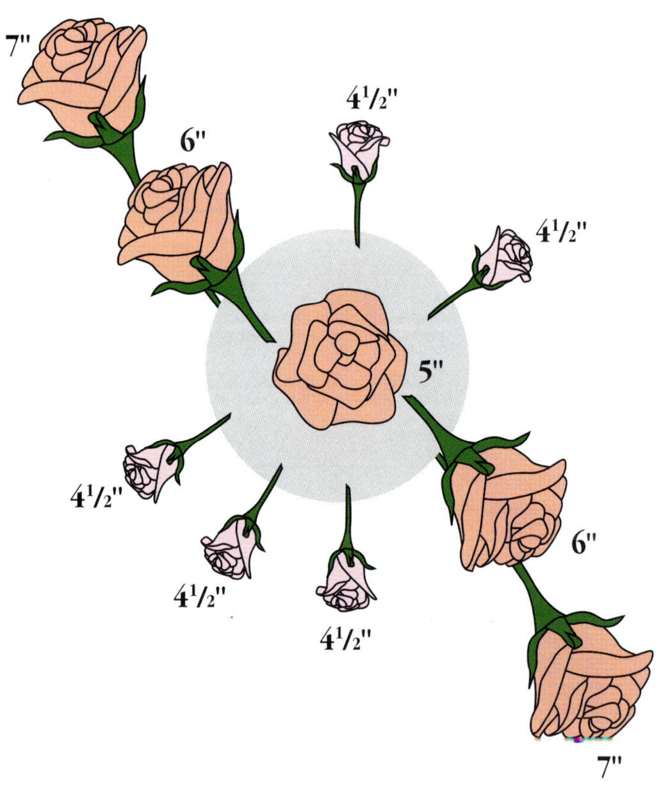

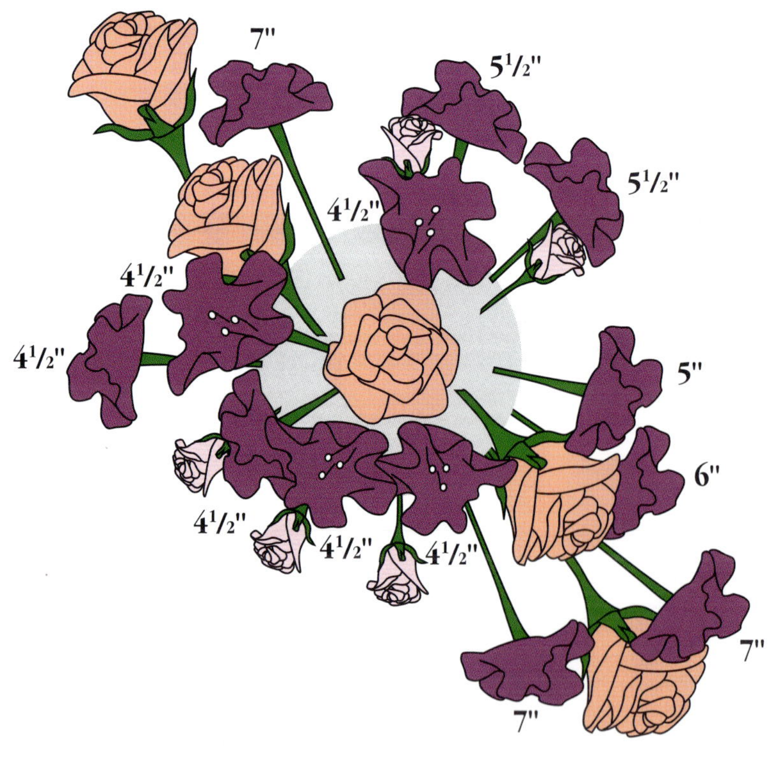

VARIATION
Materials Used:
Bouquet holder; 8" lace collar; **FOCAL:** 3 lilies; **SECONDARY:** 12 carnations, 6 mini rosebuds; **FILLER:** 30 heather sprigs, 3 lily buds, preserved plumosus fern; 1 yd of #5 lace ribbon.

SOPHISTICATE ATTENDANT'S BOUQUET

ROMANCE

Approximate size: 11" round

This basic round shape is the most commonly used for Attendants' bouquets due to its stylish simplicity. The symmetry is easy to establish since all stem lengths are approximately the same, thereby making it an easy design to make. Keep the face of a clock in mind when assembling this bouquet. A variety of FILLERS, such as baby's breath, preserved gypsophilia, tulle puffs, or ribbon loops, may be used to accent this design.

Familiarize yourself with the information found on pgs. 2-11. Stem lengths indicated are measured from the TOP of blossom, leaf, or preserved material and include 1" to be inserted into foam base.

MATERIALS

Bouquet holder; 8" lace collar; **FOCAL:** 9 roses; **FILLER:** 30 azalea blossoms with leaves, 8 pearl loops, 7 clusters of satin phlox, 1$\frac{1}{3}$ yds of #1 ribbon; 4 yds of 6"w tulle.

ASSEMBLY INSTRUCTIONS

1. Place holder into lace collar.

2. Prepare and stem materials, referring to diagram and as follows:
   Azalea blossoms — thirty 4$\frac{1}{2}$"
   Pearl loops — eight 5"
   Phlox clusters — seven 4$\frac{1}{2}$"
3. Insert roses, referring to diagram for placement.
4. Insert azalea blossoms around roses.
5. Cut six 8" lengths of ribbon. Make into 6 loops.
6. Accent with phlox clusters, pearl loops, and ribbon loops.
7. Cut sixteen 9" lengths of tulle. Stack 2 lengths; fold in half. Hand gather long raw edges; stem. Repeat with remaining tulle lengths. Insert between lace collar and flowers.

5" 5" 5" 5" 5" 5" 5" 5" 5"

KEY
Rose

VARIATION
Materials Used:
Bouquet holder; 8" lace collar; **FOCAL:** 5 dark carnations, 10 light carnations; **FILLER:** 11 small rosebuds, 16 azalea leaf clusters, 11 dried baby's breath clusters; 1$\frac{3}{4}$ yds of #9 ribbon.

ROMANCE ATTENDANT'S BOUQUET

LOVING EMBRACE

Approximate size: 12" wide x 15" long

This basic oval-shaped Attendant's bouquet is an ideal way to use varying shades of the same color with a variety of flower types and sizes. The look is that of flowing movement — a natural, airy appearance.

Familiarize yourself with the information found on pgs. 2-11. Stem lengths indicated are measured from the TOP of blossom, leaf, or preserved material and include 1" to be inserted into foam base.

MATERIALS

Bouquet holder; 8" lace collar; **FOCAL:** 8 calla lilies; **SECONDARY:** 9 dark lilac spikes, 5 light lilac spikes; **FILLER:** 6 embroidered leaves, 36 ivy sprigs, 4 crystal bead sprays, preserved plumosus fern.

ASSEMBLY INSTRUCTIONS

1. Place holder into lace collar.
2. Prepare and stem materials, referring to diagrams and as follows:

   Embroidered leaves — six $4^1/_2$"
   Ivy clusters (3 sprigs each)— four 4" and eight $4^1/_2$"
   Bead sprays — four $4^1/_2$"
   Plumosus fern clusters (5 sprigs each) — four 5"

3. Insert calla lilies and lilacs, referring to diagrams for placement.
4. Insert ivy clusters around flowers.
5. Accent with plumosus fern clusters, embroidered leaves, and bead sprays.

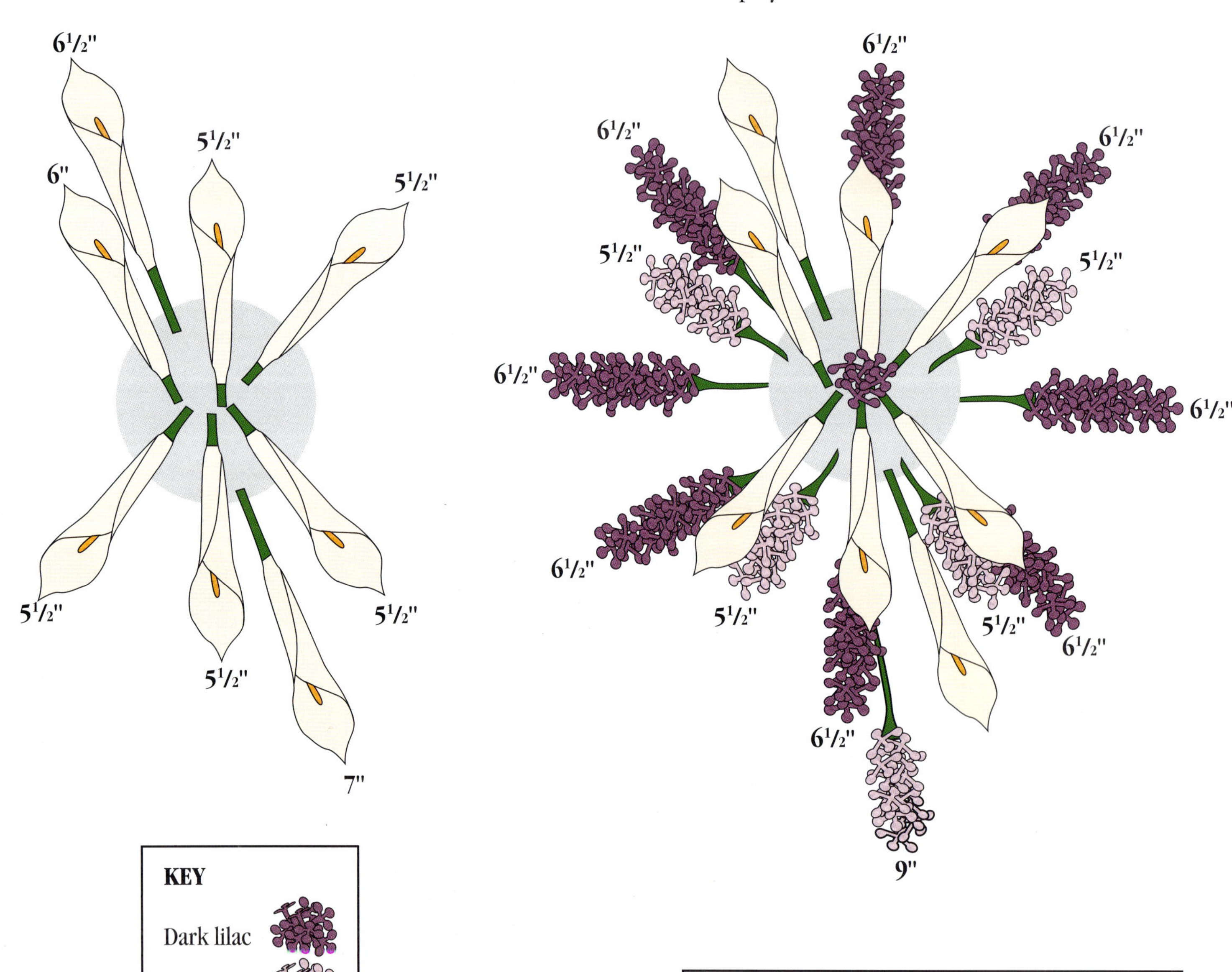

VARIATION
Materials Used:
Bouquet holder; 8" lace collar; **FOCAL:** 10 carnations, 9 roses; **SECONDARY:** 16 lilac spikes; **FILLER:** 2 medium rosebuds, 32 heather spikes, 12 maidenhair fern clusters.

31

LOVING EMBRACE ATTENDANT'S BOUQUET

THE LANGUAGE OF ROMANCE

Approximate size: 12" wide x 22" long

The use of unusual accents such as ting-ting, along with interesting floral combinations, makes this easy-to-do hand-wrapped Attendant's bouquet especially appealing. The sturdy stems of the FOCAL flowers serve as the handle for this dramatic style.

Familiarize yourself with the information found on pgs. 2-11. Stem lengths indicated are measured from the TOP of blossom, leaf, or preserved material.

MATERIALS

FOCAL: 3 roses; **SECONDARY:** 5 lilac spikes; **FILLER:** preserved plumosus fern; $2^2/_3$ yds of 6"w tulle.

ASSEMBLY INSTRUCTIONS

1. Prepare and stem materials, referring to diagrams and as follows:

    Plumosus fern — 10 clusters ranging from 10" to 17" tall with 7-10 sprigs per cluster

2. The 22" rose will be the main stem. Add the other roses to the main stem, taping at the tape point and referring to diagram for placement. Bend stems as desired.
3. Tape lilac stems to main stem, referring to diagram for placement. Bend stems as desired.
4. Tape plumosus fern clusters around lilacs, taping at the tape point.
5. Cut a 60" length of tulle for bow; set aside.
6. To create the handle, start at tape point and wrap the stems from top to bottom with remaining tulle; glue.
7. Use 60" length of tulle to make a 6-loop bow with 5" loops; glue bow to top of tape point.

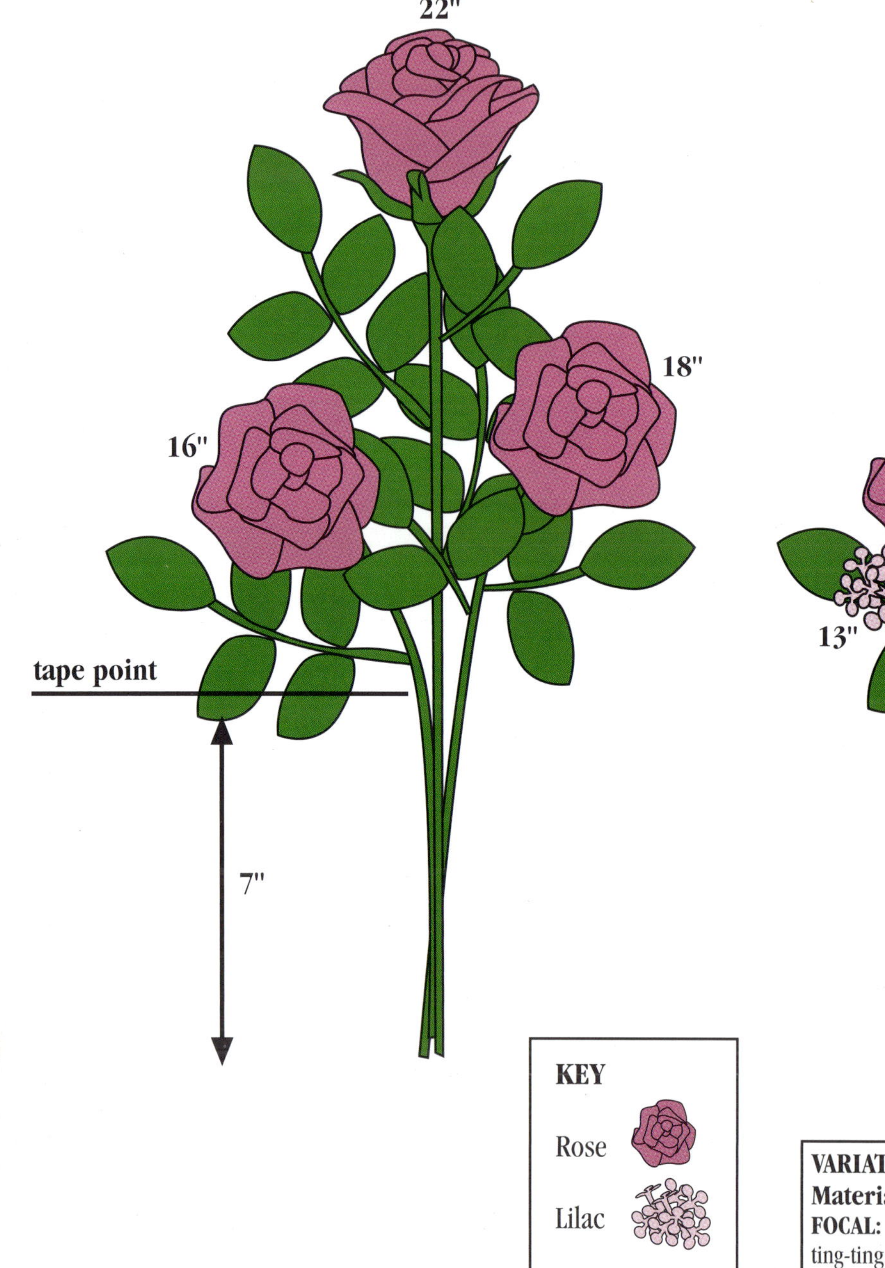

KEY

Rose

Lilac

VARIATION
Materials Used:
FOCAL: 5 magnolia blossoms; **SECONDARY:** 5 stock spikes; **FILLER:** curly ting-ting, 19" leaf stem with 9 leaves; $2^2/_3$ yds of 6"w tulle.

THE LANGUAGE OF ROMANCE ATTENDANT'S BOUQUET

ROMANTIC SERENADE

Approximate size: 17" wide x 16$^{1}/_{2}$" long

So much can be done with the romantic ivy vine. In these lovely Attendant's bouquets, the sturdy stem of the ivy bush is used as the base instead of using a bouquet holder. This hand-wrapped style allows you to use large FOCAL flowers to make a dramatic statement.

Familiarize yourself with the information found on pgs. 2-11. Stem lengths indicated are measured from the TOP of blossom, leaf, or preserved material.

MATERIALS

LINE: ivy bush with 14 stems; **FOCAL:** 3 lilies, 3 daisies; **FILLER:** 2 lily buds, 5 magnolia blossoms, 6 heather spikes; 3 yds of #9 ribbon.

ASSEMBLY INSTRUCTIONS

1. Prepare and stem materials, referring to diagrams and as follows:
   Lily buds — one 13" and one 15"
   Magnolias — one 10", two 12$^{1}/_{2}$", one 13", and one 14"
   Heather spikes — one 11", two 13", two 14", and one 16$^{1}/_{2}$"

2. Tape lilies and daisies to ivy bush stem, referring to diagrams for placement. Bend stems as desired.
3. Tape magnolias, heather spikes, and lily buds to ivy bush stem. Bend stems as desired.
4. Cut a 76" length of ribbon for bow; set aside.
5. To create the handle, start at top of ivy bush stem and wrap the stems from top to bottom with remaining ribbon; glue.
6. Use 76" length of ribbon to make an 8-loop bow with 3$^{1}/_{2}$" loops and two 9" streamers; glue bow to handle.

VARIATION
Materials Used:
LINE: ivy bush with 14 stems; **FOCAL:** 3 magnolia blossoms, 6 ranunculus blossoms; **FILLER:** 6 hops spikes, 1 magnolia bud, 3 ranunculus buds; 3 yds of #9 ribbon.

ROMANTIC SERENADE ATTENDANT'S BOUQUET

LACE FAN

Approximate size: 14" wide x 10" high

*A delicate lace fan makes a lovely backdrop for an Attendant's bouquet.
There are several styles of fans available that have a foam center and can be used as a bouquet.*

Familiarize yourself with the information found on pgs. 2-11. Stem lengths indicated are measured from the TOP of blossom, preserved material, or leaf and include 1" to be inserted into foam base.

MATERIALS

10" lace wedding fan with foam center; **FOCAL:** 3 roses; **FILLER:** 19 azalea blossoms with leaves, 7 mini rosebuds, 26 sprigs of silk baby's breath; 2 yds of #9 ribbon.

ASSEMBLY INSTRUCTIONS

1. Glue foam center into fan; wrap with wire to secure.
2. Prepare and stem materials, referring to diagram and as follows:
   Azalea — eight 3", four 4", three 4½", and four 5"
   Baby's breath clusters (2 sprigs each) — seven 4", four 5", and two 7"
3. Insert roses and rosebuds, referring to diagram for placement.
4. Insert azalea blossoms around roses and rosebuds.
5. Accent with baby's breath clusters.

6. Make an 8-loop bow with 2½" loops and two 10" streamers from ribbon. Cut an 11" length of ribbon; make a loop. Insert bow and loop in bottom of bouquet.

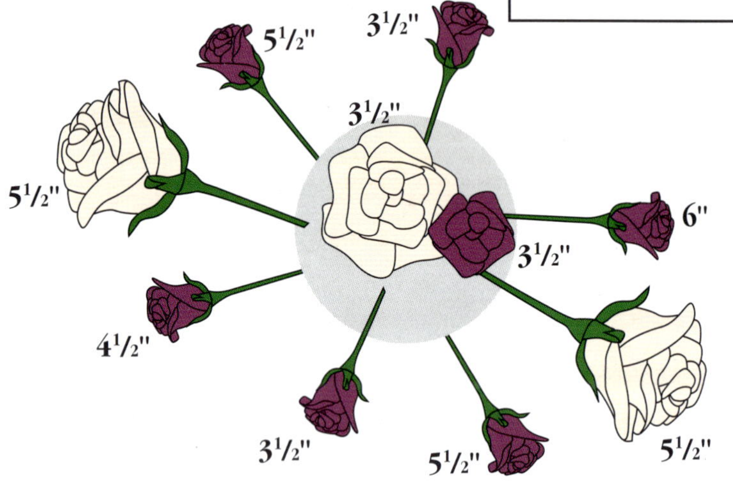

BIBLE COVER

Approximate size: 5½" wide x 9" long

*There are many interesting items on which flower sprays can be placed, and items with lacy backgrounds
are among the most popular. Parasols, Bible covers, and video covers all make ideal complementary accessories.*

Familiarize yourself with the information found on pgs. 2-11. Stem lengths indicated are measured from the TOP of blossom, preserved material, or leaf.

MATERIALS

Bible cover; **FOCAL:** 3 magnolia blossoms with leaves; **FILLER:** 5 magnolia buds, 1¼ yds of 6"w tulle, dried baby's breath; 2¼ yds of satin tubing.

ASSEMBLY INSTRUCTIONS

1. Stem all flowers and fillers on floral wire so that the stems are approximately 4" long, making 7 tulle puffs and 7 clusters of baby's breath with 4 sprigs each.
2. Cut two 7" lengths of tubing. Insert floral wire into lengths. Form each length into a single tubing loop.
3. Using corsage method, make flower spray, referring to diagram for placement.
4. Cut a 14", an 11", and a 9" length of tubing. Form lengths into one multiple loop.
5. Insert floral wire into remaining tubing. Make an 8-loop bow with 2" loops from this tubing.

6. Glue flower spray to front of Bible cover.
7. Glue bow and multiple loop to Bible cover along lower left side of spray.

LACE FAN

BIBLE COVER

GARDEN BASKET

Approximate size: 14" x 18"

A basket filled with beautiful blooms makes a charming Attendant's bouquet.

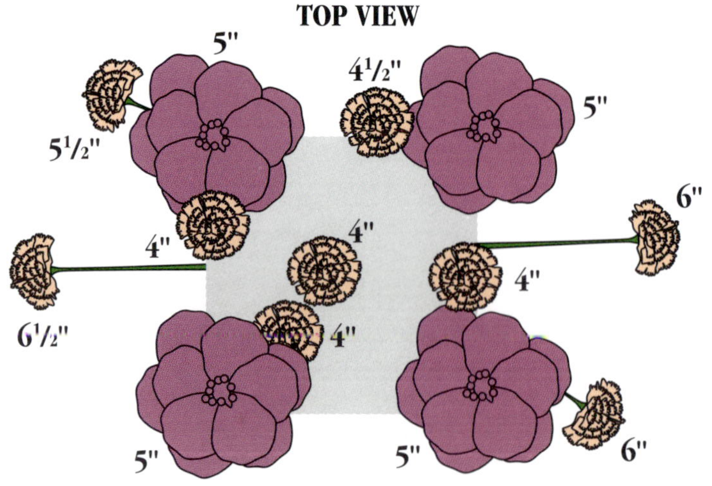

Familiarize yourself with the information found on pgs. 2-11. Stem lengths indicated are measured from the TOP of blossom, preserved material, or leaf and include 1" to be inserted into foam base.

MATERIALS

10"w x 12"l x 8"h basket; **FOCAL:** 4 poppies; **LINE:** 14 ivy stems; **SECONDARY:** 9 carnations, 11 pansies; **FILLER:** 4 poppy buds, 5 pansy buds, 21 heather spikes, 1½ yds of 3"w lace; 1½ yds of #3 ribbon; 4" square of foam.

ASSEMBLY INSTRUCTIONS

1. Glue and wire the foam piece in center of basket.
2. Cut six 9" lengths of lace. Make 6 lace fans.
3. Prepare and stem materials, referring to diagram and as follows:

   Ivy — three 4", two 5", four 6", three 7", and two 10"
   Pansies — three 4", five 5", and three 7"
   Poppy buds — three 5" and one 6"
   Pansy buds — three 4" and two 5"
   Heather — one 3", ten 5", six 6", two 7" one 8", and one 9"

4. Insert poppies and carnations, referring to diagram for placement.

5. Insert ivy, allowing some pieces to cascade out of basket. Insert remaining flowers, placing longer stems toward outer edges.

6. Make a 4-loop bow with 1½' loops and three 9" streamers from ribbon. Make a tiny loop and glue to center of bow. Glue bow to front of basket.

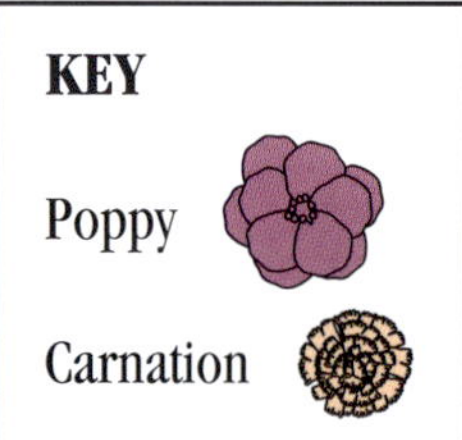

TOP VIEW

FLOWERED WREATH

Approximate size: 13" round

For a unique Attendant's bouquet, here's a wreath of garden flowers. The wreath symbolizes everlasting love and echoes the shape of the wedding bands to be exchanged by the Bride and Groom.

MATERIALS

12" diameter foam wreath; **FOCAL:** 3 large roses, 2 medium roses; **SECONDARY:** 14 small rosebuds; **FILLER:** 5 dogwood blossoms, hydrangea bloom with 22 blossoms, 10 mini eucalyptus stems, 7 sprigs of mini berries, 12 large rose leaves, 3¾ yds of 2"w lace; 6 yds of 6"w tulle.

ASSEMBLY INSTRUCTIONS

1. Wrap wreath with tulle, being sure to completely cover foam. Secure tulle with glue.
2. Arrange and glue rose leaves on front of wreath, overlapping as necessary.
3. Trim eucalyptus stems to approximately 4" long. Remove remaining flower heads from stems.
4. Glue large roses, medium roses, and rosebuds to wreath, referring to diagram for placement.
5. Glue remaining flowers, berries, and greenery to wreath.
6. Cut eight 8" lengths of lace. Make 8 lace fans; glue to wreath.
7. Cut a 15" length of lace. Fold length of lace in half for carrying loop. Pin and glue ends of loop to top center of wreath.
8. Cut a 50" length of lace. Make an 8-loop bow with 2½" loops and two 3" streamers. Turn ends of streamers to wrong side and glue in place. Pin and glue bow to front of wreath, covering ends of carrying loop.

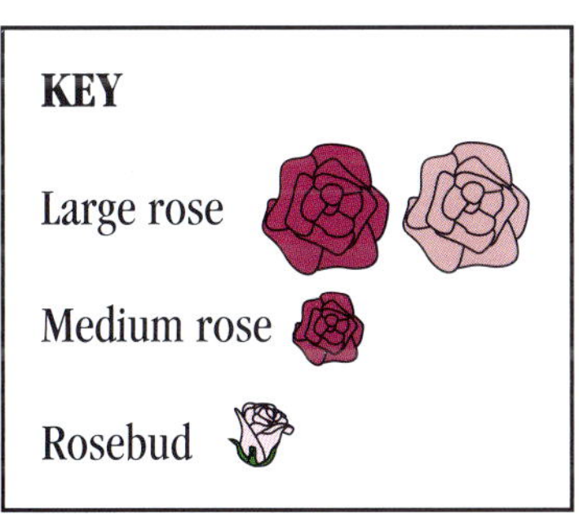

HEADPIECES

Headpieces may be worn by the Bride or Attendants, with or without veils. With the wide variety of ready-made veils and poufs available, any of these lovely headpieces can be made quickly and easily. Flowers should coordinate with those in bouquets, and ribbon streamers may be added to the back of an Attendant's headpiece. Consider the height of the Groom when determining the height of the pouf for the Bride's veil. Most Brides don't want to tower over their Grooms.

VEIL WITH BEADED HEADBAND

MATERIALS

17" x 24" bridal veil with blusher, pearl beaded headband, sewing needle and sewing thread to match veil.

ASSEMBLY INSTRUCTIONS

1. Adjust size of veil to measure 4" by pulling drawstring; secure with small basting stitches.
2. Apply thin line of glue to headband. Glue veil to headband.

WREATH VEIL

MATERIALS

17" x 24" veil with corded pouf, 1 flowered bridal wreath, ⅓ yd of #3 ribbon.

ASSEMBLY INSTRUCTIONS

1. Adjust wreath to fit Bride's head. Glue pouf line of veil to back of flowered wreath.
2. Glue ribbon over glue line at back of veil.

PADDED SATIN HEADBAND

MATERIALS

Padded satin headband, 10" pearl bridal spray, 1 pearl bridal flower, ½ yd of #9 ribbon.

ASSEMBLY INSTRUCTIONS

1. Use ribbon to make a 6-loop bow with 1½" loops; glue to side of headband.
2. Glue pearl spray behind bow; glue pearl flower to center of bow.

WREATH VEIL
PADDED SATIN HEADBAND

HATS

The Bride's hat should always complement her gown and be accented with flowers matching those in her bouquet. Our versatile large-brimmed hat can be worn several ways. When Attendants are to wear hats, they should be smaller than the Bride's.

PILLBOX HAT

MATERIALS

Pillbox hat, corded tulle bridal pouf, 4 embroidered leaves, sewing needle and sewing thread to match tulle pouf.

ASSEMBLY INSTRUCTIONS

1. Adjust size of tulle pouf to fit hat by pulling the drawstring; secure with small basting stitches.
2. Apply thin line of glue to hat where pouf is to be attached. Glue pouf to hat.
3. Glue embroidered leaves over glue line.

BRIDAL HAT

MATERIALS

Large-brimmed bridal hat, 1 large satin rose with leaves, 2 embroidered leaves, 2 stems of satin bridal flowers, 2 pearl sprays.

ASSEMBLY INSTRUCTIONS

1. Bend up one side of brim to crown; glue to secure.
2. Remove rose head and leaves from stem.
3. Glue rose, leaves, bridal flowers, and pearl sprays to brim.

BRIDAL HAT

HAIR ACCESSORIES

These accents either match the Attendants' gowns or are an extension of their bouquets. Consider hair length when determining a style suitable to all. Pearls, tulle puffs, or ribbons color-coordinated with the gowns or bouquets may be incorporated with the flowers.

ROSEBUD CLUSTER

ROSEBUD CLUSTER

Approximate Size: 2 ½" x 3 ½"

Familiarize yourself with the information found on pgs. 2-11.

MATERIALS

For each cluster, you will need: 1 small rosebud, 2 azalea buds with leaves, 1 pearl loop, and 1 cluster of satin phlox.

ASSEMBLY INSTRUCTIONS

1. Stem all materials on floral wire so that the stems are approximately 4" long.
2. Refer to diagram and form a cluster with all materials, placing rosebud in center and surrounding it with other materials; tape together.
3. Attach to hair with hairpins.

BABY'S BREATH

Approximate size: 7"

Familiarize yourself with the information found on pgs. 2-11.

MATERIALS

1 hair comb, 1 stem of silk baby's breath.

ASSEMBLY INSTRUCTIONS

1. Stem 1 baby's breath cluster on a 7" floral wire stem.
2. Use cascade method to make spray, using 6 more clusters of baby's breath.
3. Glue flower spray to comb. Bend and shape stem as desired.

POUF

Approximate size: 7"

MATERIALS

1 hair comb, 8 lilac blossoms, 1 tulle bridal pouf, 11 pearls.

ASSEMBLY INSTRUCTIONS

1. Glue comb to center of tulle pouf.
2. Glue lilac blossoms to comb and to tulle; glue pearls to tulle as desired.

SATIN FLOWERS

Approximate Size: 5" x 6"

MATERIALS

3 stems satin bridal flowers with pearl centers.

ASSEMBLY INSTRUCTIONS

1. Holding all stems together, tape stems together below lowest blossom.
2. Bend stems as desired.
3. Attach to hair with hairpins.

BRIDE'S THROW BOUQUET

*The simple round throw bouquet accented with cascading ribbons will be a valued keepsake
for the person who catches it! This bouquet is also perfect for the bride to carry at the wedding rehearsal.*

Familiarize yourself with the information found on pgs. 2-11.
Stem lengths indicated are measured from the TOP of blossom,
preserved material, or leaf and include 1" to be inserted into
foam base.

MATERIALS

Bouquet holder; 8" lace collar; **FOCAL:** 6 carnations; **FILLER:** 60"
of 6"w tulle, 7 clusters of satin phlox, 6 pearl sprays, 12 green
leaves; 16 satin phlox blossoms; 2 yds of #1 ribbon.

ASSEMBLY INSTRUCTIONS

1. Cut a 13", a 12", an 11", a 10", and an 8" length of ribbon.
   Glue phlox blossoms to ribbon lengths as desired.
2. Place holder into lace collar.
3. Prepare and stem materials, referring to diagram and as
   follows:

   Tulle puffs — 10 with 3" stems
   Phlox clusters — seven 3"
   Pearl sprays — 6 with 3" stems

Leaves — twelve 2¹⁄₂"

4. Insert carnations, referring to diagram for placement.
5. Insert tulle puffs, phlox clusters, pearl sprays, and leaves
   around carnations.
6. Stem and insert ribbon
   lengths into bottom of
   bouquet.

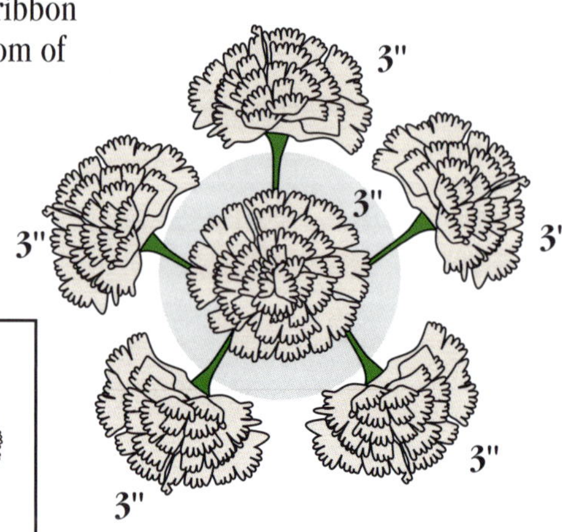

SINGLE-FLOWER CORSAGES

*Select a good-quality silk flower from the wide array of styles and colors available for the Single-Flower corsage.
The single FOCAL flower will give an air of sophisticated elegance as it is worn on the lapel, at the neckline, at the waist,
or attached to a handbag. Backgrounds can be buds, ferns, laces, tulle, or exotic leaves, and the corsage can be accented with
simple pearl or ribbon trims. Any of these corsages would make a lovely wrist corsage by attaching it to a wristlet.*

GENERAL ASSEMBLY FOR ALL CORSAGES

Familiarize yourself with the information found on pgs. 2-11.
Referring to Assembly diagram, use corsage method to assemble
materials.

MATERIALS

ORCHID
FOCAL: 1 orchid; **FILLER:**
5 tulle puffs, 3 green leaves;
BOW: ⁷⁄₈ yd of #3 ribbon made
into an 8-loop bow with 1¹⁄₂"
loops and two 2" streamers.

ROSE
FOCAL: 1 rose with 2 buds and
leaves; **FILLER:** 8" of 3"w lace
made into a fan; **BOW:** ⁷⁄₈ yd of #3
ribbon made into an 8-loop bow
with 1¹⁄₂" loops and two 2"
streamers.

GARDENIA
FOCAL: 1 gardenia with leaves;
FILLER: 8 tulle puffs,
5 lily-of-the-valley sprigs;
BOW: ²⁄₃ yd of #3 ribbon
made into an 8-loop
bow with 1¹⁄₂" loops.

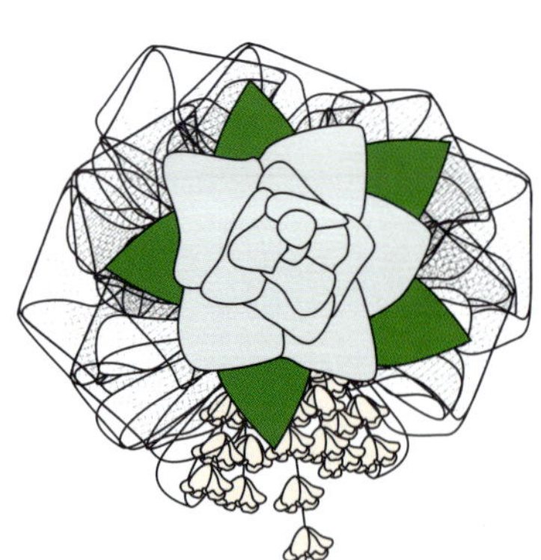

CHRYSANTHEMUM
FOCAL: 1 chrysanthemum with 2
buds; **FILLER:** 9 chrysanthemum
leaves, 6 sprigs of satin bridal
flowers; **BOW:** ⁷⁄₈ yd of #3 lace
ribbon made into an 8-loop bow
with 1¹⁄₂" loops and two 2"
streamers.

ORCHID
BRIDE'S THROW
BOUQUET
ROSE
GARDENIA
CHRYSANTHEMUM

TWO-FLOWER CORSAGES

The traditional Two-Flower corsage provides an excellent opportunity to accent with pearls, laces, ribbons, or wedding flowers. Roses are favorites for this style and make attractive wrist corsages by simply adding a corsage to a ready-made wristlet.

GENERAL ASSEMBLY FOR ALL CORSAGES

Familiarize yourself with the information found on pgs. 2-11. Referring to Assembly diagram, use corsage method to assemble materials.

MATERIALS

ORCHIDS

FOCAL: 2 orchids with 1 bud and leaves; **FILLER:** 3 leatherleaf fern fronds, 6 tulle puffs, 3 pearl sprays; **BOW:** $^2/_3$ yd of #5 ribbon made into an 8-loop bow with $1^1/_2$" loops.

BLUE ROSES

FOCAL: 2 roses with leaves; **SECONDARY:** 5 carnations, 9 clusters of satin phlox; **FILLER:** 4 small clusters of dried baby's breath; **BOW:** $^2/_3$ yd of #3 ribbon made into an 8-loop bow with $1^1/_2$" loops.

BLACK ROSES

FOCAL: 2 roses with leaves; **SECONDARY:** 4 lily-of-the-valley sprigs; **FILLER:** 7 tulle puffs, 12 mini berry clusters; **BOW:** $^2/_3$ yd of #1 ribbon made into an 8-loop bow with $1^1/_2$" loops.

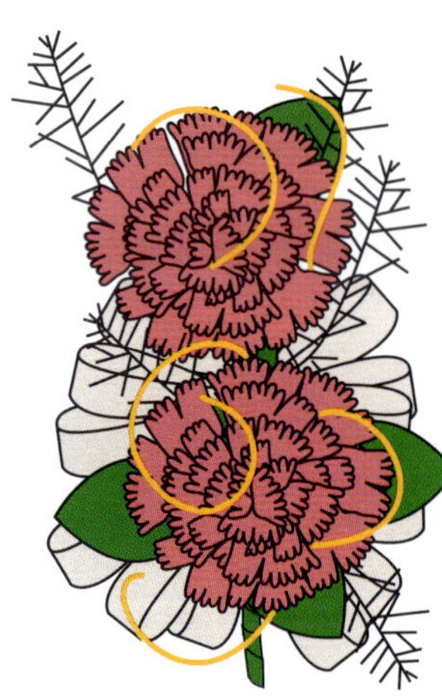

CARNATIONS

FOCAL: 2 carnations with leaves; **FILLER:** preserved plumosus fern, 5 ting-ting curls; **BOWS:** $1^1/_3$ yds of #3 ribbon made into two 8-loop bows with $1^1/_2$" loops.

BRIDE'S GARTER

The Bride's garter is a lovely accessory to be decorated with dainty flowers and greenery. Care must be taken that no wires are exposed that could tear the Bride's hosiery or clothing.

MATERIALS

Lace garter, small rosebud with leaves, 1 cluster of satin phlox, 1 pearl spray.

ASSEMBLY INSTRUCTIONS

1. Remove blossoms from stems. Separate pearl spray.
2. Glue leaves, phlox, and pearl spray pieces to rosebud, referring to diagram for placement.
3. Glue rosebud to garter.

ORCHIDS
BLACK ROSES
BRIDE'S GARTER
BLUE ROSES
CARNATIONS

MULTIPLE-FLOWER CORSAGES

The Multiple-Flower corsage is the perfect style when many flowers are desired. Small pre-assembled wedding sprays are also good to use with this design — simply back them with green leaves to show them off to their best advantage. The Multiple-Flower corsage may also be used on any video cassette tape or photograph album cover. Simply make the corsage and glue to the cover of your choice.

GENERAL ASSEMBLY FOR ALL CORSAGES

Familiarize yourself with the information found on pgs. 2-11. Referring to Assembly diagram, use corsage method to assemble materials.

MATERIALS

ZINNIAS

FOCAL: 3 zinnia blossoms with leaves and 2 zinnia buds;
BOW: 1⅛ yds of #3 ribbon made into an 8-loop bow with 2" loops and two 3" streamers.

ORCHIDS

Bible cover;
FOCAL: 5 orchids;
SECONDARY: 5 mini rosebuds with leaves;
FILLER: 5 embroidered leaves, 6 tulle puffs;
STREAMERS: 15" of #1½ ribbon folded in half.

ROSE

FOCAL: 1 rose;
SECONDARY: 5 carnations;
FILLER: 7 clusters of parsley leaves; **BOW:** 1¼ yds of decorative cording made into a 10-loop bow with 2" loops;
CORDING LOOPS: 12" of decorative cording made into a double loop, 18" of decorative cording made into a triple loop.

ROSEBUDS

FOCAL: 5 medium rosebuds;
SECONDARY: 6 clusters of silk baby's breath;
FILLER: 11 rose leaves, preserved plumosus fern, 7 crystal bead sprays;
BOW: 1⅛ yds of #3 ribbon made into an 8-loop bow with 2" loops and two 3" streamers.

DEDICATION ROSE

The single rose serves as a beautiful dedication or keepsake for your mother or any special person that you may wish to acknowledge during the ceremony.

Familiarize yourself with the information found on pgs. 2-11.

MATERIALS

FOCAL: 13" long-stem rose with leaves; **FILLER:** 3 sprigs of stephanotis, preserved plumosus fern; 2 yds of #9 ribbon.

ASSEMBLY INSTRUCTIONS

1. Stem stephanotis sprigs and 4 plumosus fern clusters with 5 sprigs each on stem wire so that stems are approximately 12" long.
2. Cluster stephanotis sprigs and plumosus fern around rose. Tape together with floral tape approximately 5" below rose blossom.
3. Cut a 46" length of ribbon. Make a 6-loop bow with 3" loops and two 5" streamers.
4. To create the handle, start at top of tape and wrap the stems from top to bottom with remaining ribbon; glue.
5. Glue bow to top of handle.

ZINNIAS
ROSE
ORCHIDS
DEDICATION ROSE
ROSEBUDS

BOUTONNIERES

The Groom's flower should match the Bride's bouquet as should the flower of the father or man escorting her down the aisle. Grandfathers of the Bride and Groom usually wear a white rose or carnation boutonniere. The boutonnieres worn by the Best Man, Groomsmen, and Ushers should coordinate with the Attendants' flowers. The Ring Bearer wears a small version to match the Groomsmen and Ushers. Boutonnieres are worn on the left lapel.

GENERAL ASSEMBLY FOR ALL BOUTONNIERES

Familiarize yourself with the information found on pgs. 2-11. Referring to Assembly diagram, use corsage method to assemble materials.

MATERIALS

CARNATION
FOCAL: 1 carnation; **FILLER:** 4 leatherleaf fern fronds, 2 green leaves.

AZALEA
FOCAL: 3 azalea blossoms with leaves; **FILLER:** 2 clusters of silk baby's breath.

LILAC
FOCAL: 1 lilac spike; **FILLER:** 2 leatherleaf fern fronds.

ORCHID
FOCAL: 2 orchids; **FILLER:** 1 azalea leaf sprig.

ROSEBUD
FOCAL: 1 large rosebud with 3 leaves; **FILLER:** 1 cluster of silk baby's breath.

STEPHANOTIS
FOCAL: 3 stephanotis blossoms; **FILLER:** preserved plumosus fern, 3 sprigs of boxwood leaves.

SWEET PEA
FOCAL: 2 sweet pea blossoms; **FILLER:** 6 mini philodendron leaves, 2 clusters of dried baby's breath.

ROSE
FOCAL: 1 rose with leaves; **FILLER:** 1 freesia stem with 3 blossoms, preserved plumosus fern.

CARNATION
LILAC
ROSEBUD
SWEET PEA
AZALEA
ORCHID
STEPHANOTIS
ROSE

LACE BASKET

The lace basket is a delicate container for a small round arrangement. It's the perfect size for a Flower Girl or Junior Attendant to carry. The basket would also make a pretty accent at the guest registry table.

Familiarize yourself with the information found on pgs. 2-11. Stem lengths indicated are measured from the TOP of blossom, preserved material, or leaf and include 1" to be inserted into foam base.

MATERIALS

Lace wedding basket with foam center; **FOCAL:** 8 azalea blossoms with leaves; **SECONDARY:** 6 small rosebuds; **FILLER:** 10 azalea buds with leaves, 8 daisies, 6 pearl loops, 8 clusters of satin phlox; 1¹/₂ yds of #1 ribbon.

ASSEMBLY INSTRUCTIONS

1. Glue foam center into basket; wrap with wire to secure.
2. Prepare and stem materials, referring to diagram and as follows:
   Azalea buds — eight 4" and two 5"
   Daisies — six 4" and two 5"
   Pearl loops — four 4" and two 5"
   Phlox clusters — eight 4"
3. Insert azaleas and rosebuds, referring to diagram for placement.
4. Insert daisies and azalea buds around flowers, placing longer stems at sides.
5. Accent with phlox and pearl loops, placing longer stems at sides.
6. Glue a length of ribbon to handle. Make a 10-loop bow with 2" loops from remaining ribbon; glue to front of handle.

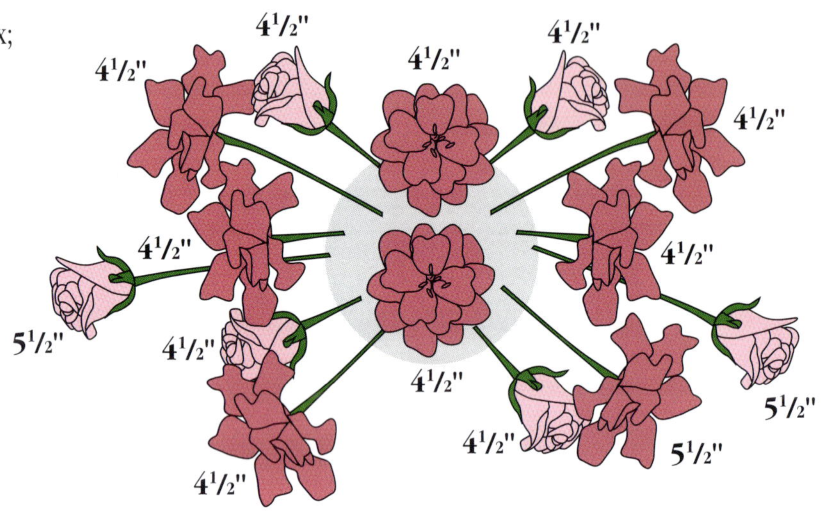

TOP VIEW

LACE PARASOL

The dainty parasol carried by the Flower Girl is fun and easy to decorate. Ribbon streamers may flow from the top since bottom trims should be kept to a minimum.

TOP SPRAY   **BOTTOM SPRAY**

Familiarize yourself with the information found on pgs. 2-11.

MATERIALS

15" tall lace parasol; **FOCAL:** 12 azalea blossoms with leaves; **SECONDARY:** 7 mini rosebuds; **FILLER:** 11 clusters of silk baby's breath; 1 yd of #9 ribbon.

ASSEMBLY INSTRUCTIONS

1. Securely knot a 6" length of ribbon around center of parasol; trim ends close to knot. Make a 6-loop bow with 2" loops from remaining ribbon; glue to parasol over knot.
2. Using corsage method, make 2 flower sprays, referring to diagrams for placement.
3. Glue each flower spray to parasol over bow.

LACE PARASOL AND LACE BASKET

FLOWER GIRL'S LILAC BALL

This charming and unusual accent is a pretty alternative to the traditional petal basket. It would be appropriate for a very young Flower Girl or for a child who feels hesitant about scattering petals in front of a large gathering.

MATERIALS

5" diameter foam ball, 12 leatherleaf fern fronds, 6 stems of light lilac, 9 dark lilac blossoms, 2 embroidered leaves, 2 crystal bead sprays, 3 ivy leaves, 1²⁄₃ yds of #2 ribbon.

ASSEMBLY INSTRUCTIONS

1. Glue leatherleaf fern fronds to foam ball, completely covering ball.
2. Separate light lilacs into blossoms.
3. Glue all lilac blossoms to fern, completely covering ball and placing dark blossoms at top of ball.
4. Cut a 50" length of ribbon. Make a 12-loop bow with 2" loops. Glue bow to top of ball.
5. Fold remaining ribbon in half to make carrying loop. Pin and glue ends of loop to ball, hiding ends in center of bow.
6. Glue embroidered leaves, ivy leaves, and crystal bead sprays to top of ball.

FLOWER GIRL'S CIRCLET

This simple wreath for the Flower Girl's hair should coordinate with the flowers the Attendants are carrying. It would also make a charming headpiece for the Attendants to wear since it looks pretty with many hairstyles.

MATERIALS

Lilac blossoms, ¹⁄₂ yd of #2 ribbon.

ASSEMBLY INSTRUCTIONS

1. Form a circle from stem wire to fit head; wrap with floral tape.
2. Cut a 7" length and a 9" length of ribbon. Glue two lilac blossoms to one end of each ribbon.
3. Glue ribbon lengths to wire circle.
4. Glue lilac blossoms to wire circle, completely covering tape and ribbon ends.

FLOWER GIRL'S LILAC BALL AND CIRCLET

PETAL BASKET

Rose petals are cut apart and placed in the petal basket for the little girl to drop along the aisle in honor of the Bride's arrival. The basket may be trimmed with ribbons and flowers that match the color scheme of the wedding and is recommended for the 3- to 6-year-old Flower Girl.

Familiarize yourself with the information found on pgs. 2-11.

MATERIALS

Lace and net wedding petal basket; **FOCAL:** 1 morning glory blossom with leaves; **SECONDARY:** 3 large rosebuds; **FILLER:** 1 morning glory bud, 2 sprigs of silk statice, 2 leatherleaf fern fronds, preserved plumosus fern; 5 roses for petals; 2 yds of #1½ ribbon.

ASSEMBLY INSTRUCTIONS

1. Glue a length of ribbon to handle.
2. Remove flower heads from stems.
3. Glue morning glory, morning glory bud, rosebuds, statice, plumosus fern, leatherleaf fern, and leaves to front of basket, referring to diagram for placement.
4. Make an 8-loop bow with 1½" loops from remaining ribbon; glue bow to bottom of basket.
5. Cut roses into separate petals and place inside basket.

ROSE CLUSTER BOUQUET

This simple bouquet has a variety of uses. Not only would it make
a pretty Junior Attendant's bouquet, it could also be used as the Bride's throw bouquet.
It could even serve as a casual arrangement when placed on a serving table.

Familiarize yourself with the information found on pgs. 2-11. Stem lengths indicated are measured from the TOP of blossom, preserved material, or leaf.

MATERIALS

8" lace collar, 12 roses, 6 rose leaves, 4 yds of 6"w tulle, 3 yds of #3 ribbon.

ASSEMBLY INSTRUCTIONS

1. Stem all roses and leaves on stem wire so that the stems are approximately 12" long.
2. Holding all stems in one hand, arrange roses in a round cluster. Tape stems together 6" from bottom of stems. Add rose leaves around base of roses; tape all stems together.
3. Place stems into lace collar. Do not cut off plastic prongs on lace collar.
4. Starting at bottom of collar and covering plastic prongs, securely tape lace collar to stems.
5. Cut a 96" length of tulle. Make a 12-loop bow with 4" loops.
6. Starting at bottom of collar, wrap stems with remaining tulle; glue.
7. Use ribbon to make a 7-loop bow with 3" loops and six 11" streamers.
8. Glue tulle bow to center front of bouquet. Glue ribbon bow to center of tulle bow.

RING BEARER'S PILLOWS

The designs used on the pillow are similar to a small corsage and are coordinated with the Flower Girl's flowers. Any rings used on the pillow should be artificial. Since the Ring Bearer is usually a young child, flowers and rings should be securely glued or sewn to the pillow and not pinned.

Familiarize yourself with the information found on pgs. 2-11.

BUTTERFLY

MATERIALS

Square satin pillow; **FOCAL:** 2 large rosebuds with leaves; **SECONDARY:** 2 morning glory blossoms; **FILLER:** 1 morning glory bud, 2 leatherleaf fern fronds, preserved plumosus fern, 1 cluster of silk statice; 2 rings; $1^7/_8$ yds of #2 ribbon.

ASSEMBLY INSTRUCTIONS

1. Use ribbon to make an 8-loop bow with 2" loops and three 5" streamers.
2. Using corsage method, make flower spray, referring to diagram for placement.
3. To create the butterfly, knot an 18" length of ribbon around center of pillow.
4. Glue flower spray to pillow.
5. Glue rings to pillow.

HEART

MATERIALS

Heart-shaped satin pillow; **FOCAL:** 1 calla lily; **FILLER:** 2 embroidered leaves, preserved plumosus fern, 4 ivy leaves, 3 crystal bead sprays; 2 rings; $1^1/_2$ yds of #2 ribbon.

ASSEMBLY INSTRUCTIONS

1. Use ribbon to make an 8-loop bow with 2" loops and three 6" streamers.
2. Using corsage method, make flower spray, referring to diagram for placement.
3. Glue flower spray to pillow.
4. Tie rings to one streamer.

SQUARE

MATERIALS

Square satin pillow; **FOCAL:** 3 roses; **SECONDARY:** 2 azalea clusters with 3 buds and leaves; **FILLER:** 2 statice blossoms, 2 clusters of satin phlox, 2 pearl loops; 2 rings; 15" of #1 ribbon.

ASSEMBLY INSTRUCTIONS

1. Using corsage method, make flower spray, referring to diagram for placement.
2. Glue flower spray to pillow.
3. Cut ribbon length in half. Tie rings to ribbons. Glue ribbons to pillow; trim ribbon ends as desired.

BUTTERFLY
HEART
SQUARE

PEW BOWS

Approximate size: 11" round

Large bows, often decorated with greenery or flower sprays, indicate special seating of immediate family members and may be made in colors to complement the wedding flowers. Pew bows may also be used at other locations along the aisle, but such bows should be smaller and without added decoration. White or ivory pew bows may also be used on the altar to decorate candelabras, railing, kneeling bench, or large plants.

MATERIALS

3½ yds of ribbon; optional trims: 12" x 36" length of tulle, silk flowers.

ASSEMBLY INSTRUCTIONS

1. Tape ruler or yardstick to work surface.
2. For center loop, hold end of ribbon in one hand and remainder of ribbon in other hand. Measure 5" from end of ribbon; hold at this point.
3. Holding ribbon vertically, loop longer length toward you, overlapping end 1". Gather ribbon across width and twist remaining ribbon length over so right side is facing up.

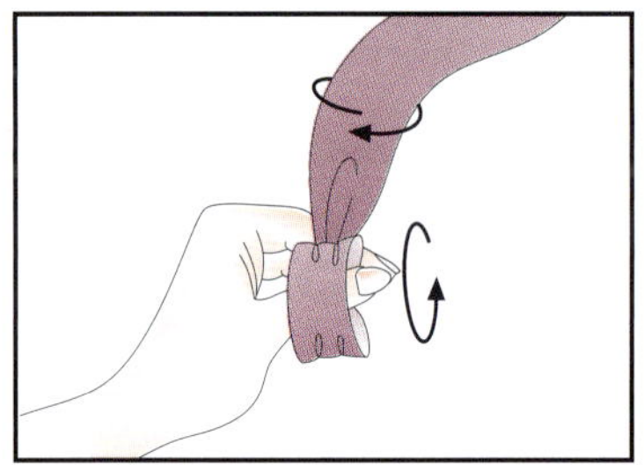

4. Measure 11" from gathered point.
5. To form next loop, loop ribbon away from you, aligning measured point with thumb and fingers of first hand. Gather points firmly in first hand. Twist remaining ribbon length over so right side of ribbon is facing up.

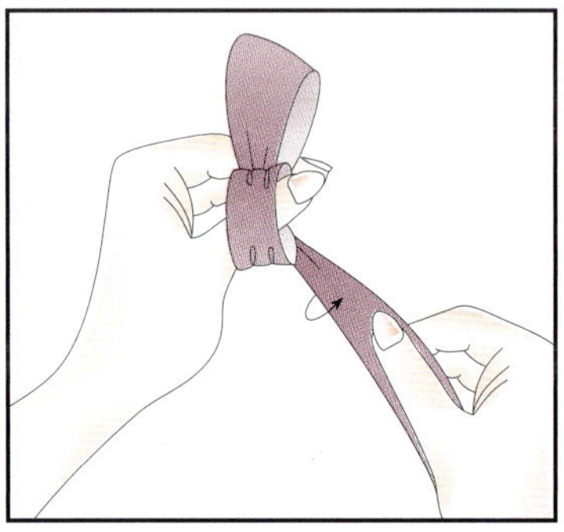

6. Measure 11" from gathered point. Loop ribbon away from you, aligning measured point with thumb and fingers of first hand. Gather points firmly in first hand. Twist remaining ribbon length over so right side of ribbon is facing up.

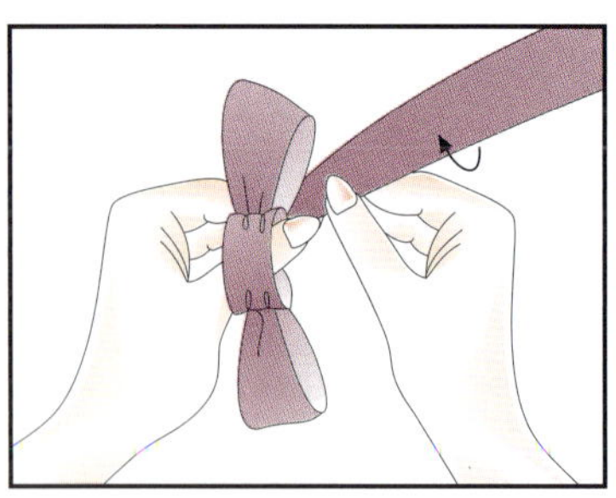

7. Repeat Steps 4-6 to continue making loops, measuring, gathering, and twisting ribbon in same manner until you have 9 loops.
8. For streamers, continue holding bow in first hand. With free hand, bring end of ribbon up to first hand and gather ribbon firmly between thumb and fingers. Cut ribbon.

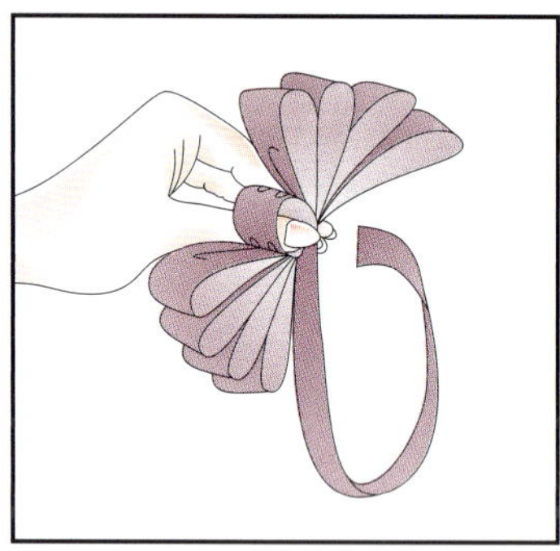

9. To secure bow, hold gathered portion with first hand and bring a length of wire around gathered portion with free hand. Hold both ends of wire together tightly behind loops. Pull loops and streamers forward away from wire and twist bow to tighten wire.

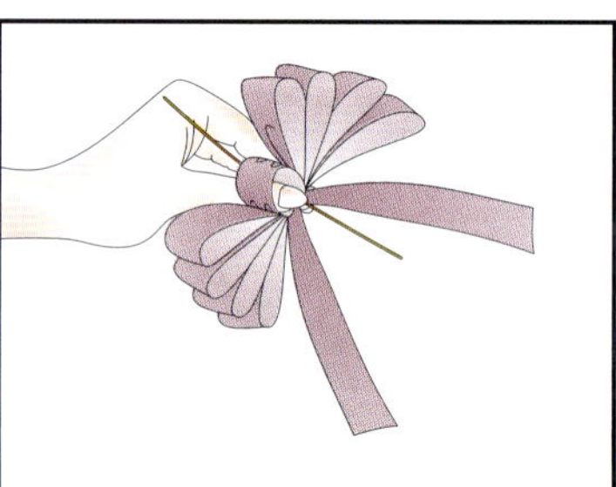

10. Spread loops open by inserting a finger at base of each loop and gently pulling outward. Arrange loops to form overall desired shape. Trim streamer ends as desired.
11. For a tulle pouf, you can gather tulle at the center and secure it with cloth-covered floral wire. Glue the tulle pouf to the center of the bow.
12. You can also glue silk flowers to the center of the bow, with or without the tulle pouf.

BASKET ALTAR ARRANGEMENT

Approximate size: 24"w x 14"d x 12"h

A pair of these bountiful baskets would look lovely on the altar table. The baskets may also be used to decorate the reception buffet tables after the ceremony. Before making your floral arrangement, check with the church to see if there are any restrictions about size, number, and color of altar arrangements.

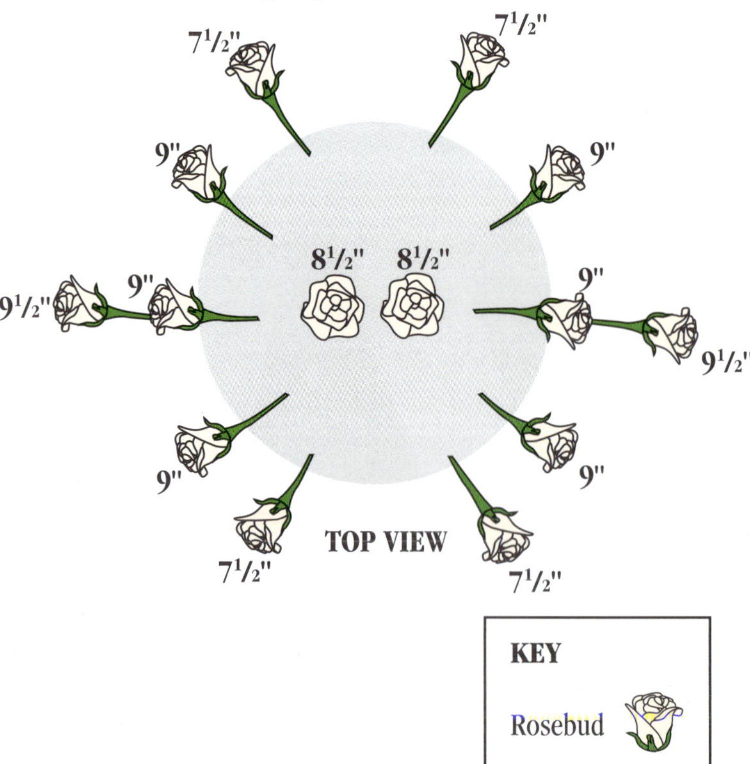

Familiarize yourself with the information found on pgs. 2-11. Stem lengths indicated are measured from the TOP of blossom, preserved material, or leaf and include 1" to be inserted into foam base.

MATERIALS

13½"w x 9"d x 11"h basket; **FOCAL:** 14 large rosebuds; **SECONDARY:** 22 azalea blossoms with leaves; **FILLER:** maple leaf bush with 32 stems, 18 azalea buds with leaves, 88 ting-ting curls; ½ of a 6" diameter foam ball; 1¾ yds of decorative cording.

ASSEMBLY INSTRUCTIONS

1. Glue the foam piece in center of basket; wrap with wire to secure.
2. Use cording to make a 4-loop bow with two 3" loops, two 2" loops, and two 10" streamers. Knot streamer ends. Wrap handle with remaining cording. Glue bow to handle.
3. Prepare and stem materials, referring to diagram and as follows:

   Azaleas — eighteen 7" and four 8"
   Maple leaf stems — thirty 6" and two 10"
   Azalea buds — sixteen 6" and two 7"
   Ting-ting curl clusters (4 curls each) — eighteen 8" and four 9"

4. Insert rosebuds, referring to diagram for placement.
5. Insert azaleas, maple leaves, and azalea buds around rosebuds, placing longer stems at sides and center.
6. Accent with ting-ting clusters.

65

TRIANGULAR ALTAR ARRANGEMENT

Approximate size: 18"w x 23"h

This simple yet elegant floral design is quite versatile. It can be used alone or paired on the altar, and it can also do double duty by serving as a decoration at the reception. Be sure to consult with the person conducting the wedding ceremony prior to the wedding regarding any restrictions regarding altar decorations.

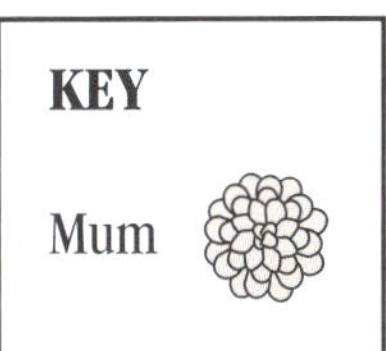

Familiarize yourself with the information found on pgs. 2-11. Stem lengths indicated are measured from the TOP of blossom, preserved material, or leaf and include 1" to be inserted into foam base.

MATERIALS

4" x 5" container; **FOCAL:** 12 large mums with leaves; **FILLER:** 54 sprigs of heather, 5 stems of leatherleaf fern with 5 fronds each; 2 yds of #40 ribbon; 4" square of foam; Spanish moss.

ASSEMBLY INSTRUCTIONS

1. Glue foam into container. Cover foam with moss.
2. Prepare and stem materials, referring to diagram and as follows:
    Heather — 8 clusters ranging from 7" to 19" tall with 2-6 sprigs per cluster
    Leatherleaf fern — two 7", one 10", one 11", and one 14"
3. Insert mums, referring to diagram for placement.
4. Insert heather clusters around mums.
5. Insert leatherleaf fern toward the back of the arrangement.
6. Use ribbon to make a 7-loop bow with a 2" center loop, six 4" loops, and two 7" streamers. Stem and insert bow in front of arrangement.

KEY

Mum

RECEPTION GUEST TABLES

A glowing candle centerpiece placed on each guest table at the reception adds charm whether you're serving traditional wedding cake and punch, buffet-style hors d'oeuvres, or a formal sit-down dinner. These attractive candle arrangements are inexpensive to make, which may be helpful when many tables are being decorated. Bud vases filled with beautiful flowers or foam hearts covered with roses provide a colorful alternative to candles.

PILLAR CANDLE WITH LACE RING

Approximate size: 8" tall x 10" diameter

Familiarize yourself with the information found on pgs. 2-11.

MATERIALS

8" tall x 3" diameter pillar candle; **FOCAL:** 4 small rosebuds; **SECONDARY:** 2 azalea blossoms with buds and leaves; **FILLER:** 2 pearl sprays; ⅔ yd of 5"w lace; 1 yd of #1 ribbon.

ASSEMBLY INSTRUCTIONS

1. To gather lace, run a 12" length of floral wire through lace 1" from one long edge. Place lace around base of candle; tighten and secure wire. (**Hint:** *Candle may be placed in an 8" saucer.*)
2. To cover wire, tie ribbon around lace, leaving 6" streamers.
3. Remove blossoms from stems. Separate pearl sprays.
4. Glue azaleas, rosebuds, and pearl spray pieces to front of candle over ribbon ends, referring to diagram for placement.

TAPER CANDLE WITH IVY VINE

Approximate size: 8" tall x 10" wide

MATERIALS

8" taper candle, glass candle holder, 18" ivy vine, 2 lilac stems, 1 yd of #9 ribbon.

ASSEMBLY INSTRUCTIONS

1. Insert candle into holder.
2. Turn 2" of each end of ribbon to wrong side; glue in place. Loosely wire the ribbon to the back of the ivy vine.
3. Separate lilac into blossoms. Glue blossoms to ivy.
4. Wrap completed ivy spray around candle holder. You may wish to glue the ivy spray to the candle holder.

PLACE CARD HOLDER

Approximate size: 5" wide

MATERIALS

1 lilac stem, 4 sprigs of ivy, 1 large ivy leaf, 20" of #9 ribbon, place card.

ASSEMBLY INSTRUCTIONS

1. Use ribbon to make a 4-loop bow with 2½" loops.
2. Separate lilac into blossoms. Glue ivy leaf sprigs and lilac blossoms to center of bow.
3. Glue ivy leaf to center back of bow. Position place card on bow. (**Hint:** *This may also be used as a favor.*)

PILLAR CANDLE WITH LACE RING

TAPER CANDLE WITH IVY VINE

PLACE CARD HOLDER

SPRINGTIME VASE

Approximate size: 20" tall

Familiarize yourself with the information found on pgs. 2-11. Stem lengths indicated are measured from the TOP of blossom, preserved material, or leaf.

MATERIALS

7½" tall bud vase; **FOCAL:** 3 alstroemeria blossoms; **LINE:** 3 larkspur spikes; **SECONDARY:** 7 azalea blossoms with leaves; **FILLER:** 4 stems of forsythia with 7 blossoms each.

ASSEMBLY INSTRUCTIONS

1. Prepare and stem materials, referring to diagram and as follows:

    Forsythia — one 11", two 12", and one 15"

2. The 20" larkspur will be the main stem in this hand-wrapped arrangement; all other flowers will be taped to this stem. The tape point will be 6" from the bottom of the main stem. Add the other larkspur to the main stem, taping at the tape point and referring to diagram for placement. Bend stems as desired.

3. Add the alstroemerias and azaleas to the main stem, taping at the tape point and referring to diagram for placement. Bend stems as desired.

4. Add forsythias to the main stem, taping at the tape point. Bend stems as desired.

5. Insert arrangement into vase.

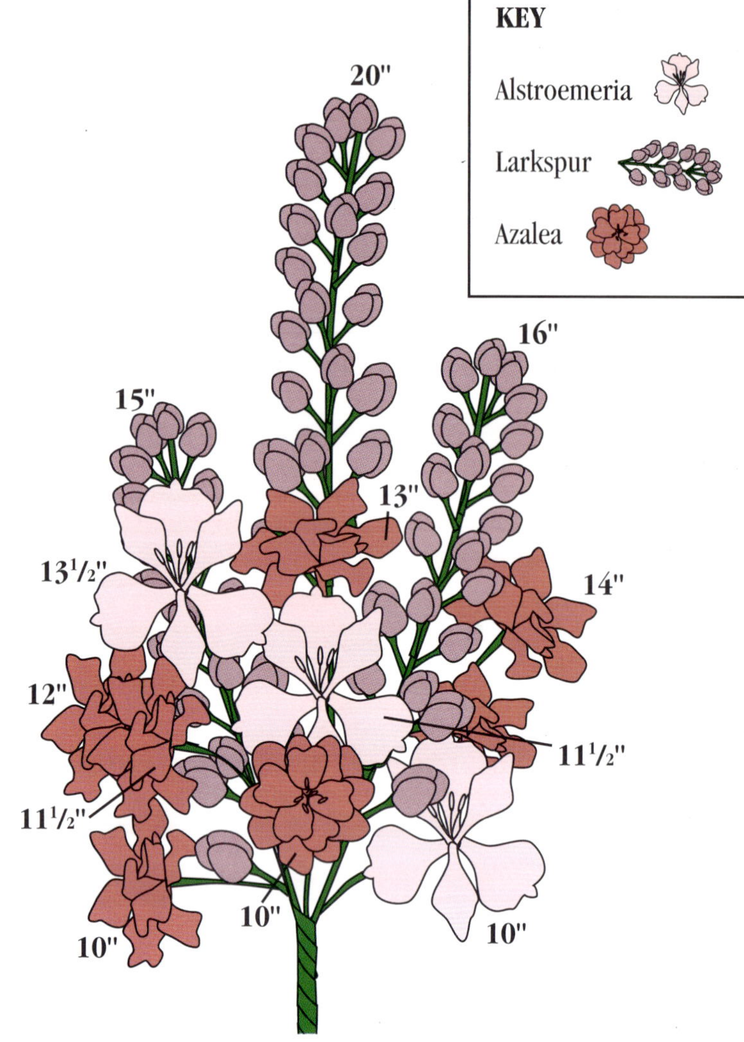

ROSEBUD VASE

Approximate size: 19" tall

Familiarize yourself with the information found on pgs. 2-11. Stem lengths indicated are measured from the TOP of blossom, preserved material, or leaf.

MATERIALS

7½" tall bud vase; **FOCAL:** 3 large rosebuds with leaves; **FILLER:** 4 heather spikes, onion grass stem; 1½ yds of #9 ribbon.

ASSEMBLY INSTRUCTIONS

1. Prepare and stem materials, referring to diagram and as follows:

    Onion grass —19"

2. The 19" rosebud will be the main stem in this hand-wrapped arrangement; all other flowers will be taped to this stem. The tape point will be 7" from the bottom of the main stem. Add the other rosebuds to the main stem, taping at the tape point and referring to diagram for placement. Bend stems as desired.

3. Add heather to the main stem, taping at the tape point and referring to diagram for placement. Bend stems as desired.

4. Add onion grass to the main stem, taping at the tape point and pulling blades of grass around flowers as desired.

5. Use ribbon to make a 6-loop bow with 3" loops and two 7" streamers; tape bow to base of flowers at top of tape point.

6. Insert arrangement into vase.

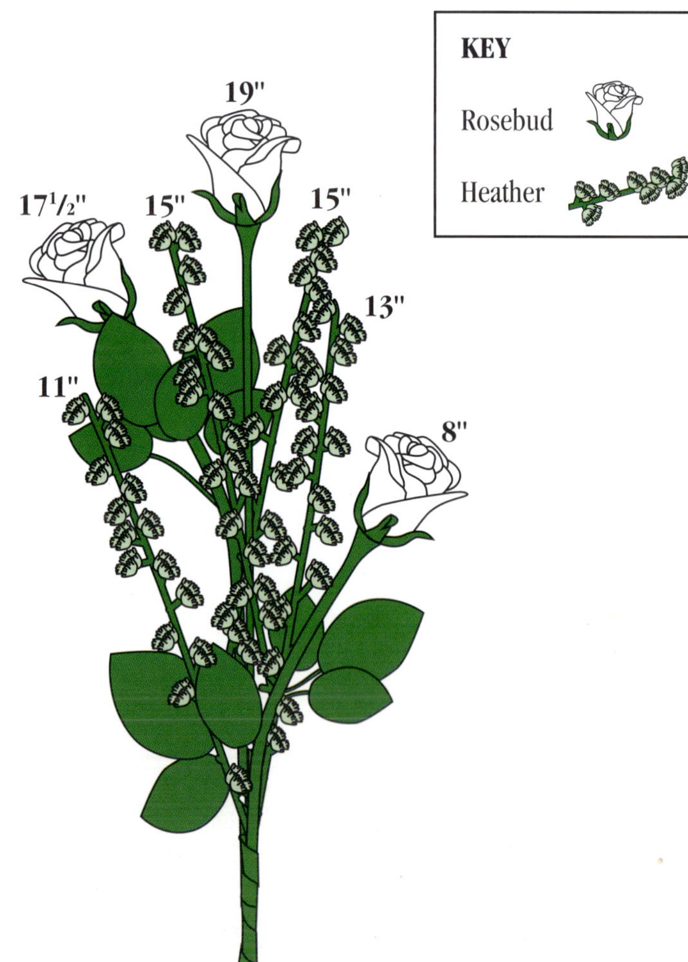

ROSE HEART

Approximate size: 6" wide

Familiarize yourself with the information found on pgs. 2-11.

MATERIALS

6"w x 1"h foam heart, 16 roses with leaves, 1 yd of #2 ribbon, 24" of #5 ribbon.

ASSEMBLY INSTRUCTIONS

1. Glue #5 ribbon around sides of heart to cover foam.
2. Remove rose heads from stems. Glue roses to top of heart, covering entire heart.
3. Accent with leaves.
4. Use remaining ribbon to make a 6-loop bow with 2" loops and two 5" streamers. Stem and insert bow in foam.

WEDDING CAKE TABLE

Serving the cake is a symbolic gesture of sharing the joy and happiness of the newlyweds with their guests. When adorning the wedding cake with flowers, the cake should be kept simple so as not to detract from the lovely flowers. Avoid the use of any flower or plant materials that could shed or break apart.

CAKE TOP

Approximate size: 9" tall

Familiarize yourself with the information found on pgs. 2-11. Stem lengths indicated are measured from the TOP of blossom, preserved material, or leaf and include 1" to be inserted into foam base.

MATERIALS

Lace caketop holder; 2½" diameter foam ball; **FOCAL:** 6 small rosebuds; **SECONDARY:** 8 azalea blossoms with leaves; **FILLER:** 6 azalea buds with leaves, 4 pearl loops, 7 clusters of satin phlox, 5 silk statice blossoms, 1 yd of 6"w tulle.

ASSEMBLY INSTRUCTIONS

1. Glue ball into caketop holder.
2. Prepare and stem materials as follows:
      Rosebuds —three 3", one 4", one 5", and one 7"
      Azaleas — four 2", two 4", and two 5½"
      Azalea buds — two 2", two 4", and two 6½"
      Pearl loops — one 2", one 4", one 5", and one 7"
      Phlox clusters — four 2", two 4", and one 6½"
      Statice — two 2", one 3", one 4", and one 6½"
      Tulle puffs — 3 with 3" stems and 2 with 4" stems
3. Insert rosebuds into ball, referring to photo for placement.
4. Insert azaleas, azalea buds, and phlox clusters, referring to photo for placement.
5. Accent with statice, tulle puffs, and pearl loops.

CHAMPAGNE GLASSES

Familiarize yourself with the information found on pgs. 2-11.

MATERIALS

2 champagne glasses; **FOCAL:** 2 small rosebuds; **SECONDARY:** 6 azalea buds with leaves; **FILLER:** 2 clusters of satin phlox, 2 silk statice blossoms, 2 pearl loops; ¾ yd of 6"w tulle; 12" of #1 ribbon.

ASSEMBLY INSTRUCTIONS

1. Stem all flowers on floral wire so that the stems are approximately 3" long.
2. For each glass, make a cluster, referring to diagram for placement.
3. Cut ribbon length in half. Glue one length of ribbon around stem of each glass.

CAKE TRIM

Familiarize yourself with the information found on pgs. 2-11.

MATERIALS

FOCAL: 9 small rosebuds; **SECONDARY:** 9 azaleas blossoms with leaves, 27 azalea buds with leaves; **FILLER:** 9 clusters of satin phlox, 9 silk statice blossoms, 9 pearl loops.

ASSEMBLY INSTRUCTIONS

1. Using cascade method, make three flower sprays, referring to diagrams for placement. The finished flower sprays should measure 7" long, 10" long, and 12" long.
2. Bend sprays to fit cake tiers. Place sprays on cake.

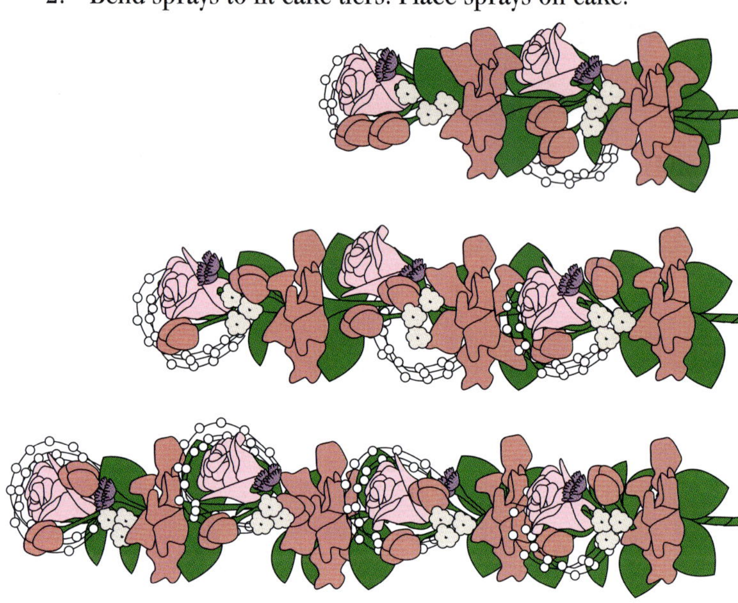

4. Glue one cluster to each glass; glue one pearl loop behind each cluster.
5. Make and glue 2 tulle puffs behind each cluster.

Continued on pg. 73.

CAKE TOP
CAKE TRIM
ATTENDANT'S
KEEPSAKE SHOE
Groom
Bride
CHAMPAGNE GLASSES
CAKE KNIFE

CAKE KNIFE

Familiarize yourself with the information found on pgs. 2-11.

MATERIALS

Cake knife; **FOCAL:** 1 small rose; **FILLER:** 3 azalea buds with leaves, 1 cluster of satin phlox,1 silk statice blossom, 1 pearl loop; ½ yd of 6"w tulle; ¾ yd of #1 ribbon.

ASSEMBLY INSTRUCTIONS

1. Cut two 6" and two 5½" lengths of ribbon. Glue ribbon streamers to side of knife handle.
2. Stem all flowers on floral wire so that the stems are approximately 3" long.
3. Make a cluster, referring to diagram for placement.
4. Glue cluster on top of ribbon streamers; glue pearl loop behind cluster.
5. Make and glue 3 tulle puffs behind cluster.

ATTENDANT'S KEEPSAKE SHOE

Here's a charming way to create a keepsake for your Attendants. Since they are unlikely to wear the shoes that match their gowns again, the flowers from their bouquets arranged in one of their shoes makes a pretty and unusual arrangement.

Familiarize yourself with the information found on pgs. 2-11.

MATERIALS

Shoe, 1½" x 4" piece of foam, Attendant's bouquet.

ASSEMBLY INSTRUCTIONS

1. Trim foam to fit inside shoe. Glue in place.
2. Remove flowers and other materials from bouquet. Insert flowers and materials into foam, restemming and trimming stems as needed.

Dresses furnished by **Just For Tonight, Inc.**, Little Rock, Arkansas, specializing in evening wear rentals and custom attendants' attire.